NOTES

OF

A TOUR

FROM

CALCUTTA TO DELHI,

IN JANUARY, 1853.

BY

THE REV. J. LONG.

CALCUTTA:

PRINTED BY SANDERS, CONES AND CO., NO. 14, LOLL BAZAR.

1853.

THE GRAND TRUNK ROAD—ITS LOCALITIES.

[FROM THE CALCUTTA REVIEW, NO. XLI.]

1. *Joseph's Map of the Grand Trunk Road, from Calcutta to Benares.*
2. *Ditto Ditto, from Benares to Agra.*
3. *Sherwill's Geological Map of the Districts North and South of the Grand Trunk Road, between Calcutta and Allahabad. 1853. 8 Rupees. Surveyor General's Office.*

WE have lately directed the reader's attention to *Calcutta in the Olden Time;* and now start from the city of palaces to Delhi, along a route which calls up vivid associations of the past, along with a view of nature, always blooming amid the ruins of man's handy work.

Our article is not designed so much for the information of Mofussilites, who are, or ought to be, familiar with the facts we shall state; but for those residents in Calcutta and its neighbourhood, or those strangers from England, who wish, in the absence of a North India " Murray " to have a descriptive outline of a country they propose to visit for health or business, and who are anxious to obtain hints and references suggestive of further inquiry—to know what can be seen in a tour of six weeks to the North West Provinces, at an outlay of 400 rupees. In 1850 a single seat from Calcutta to Benares cost 165 rupees, now it costs only 140 rupees from *Calcutta* to *Meerut.* We do not write for those who wish to make a tour in the mode of the London Cockney, " getting over the greatest possible amount of ground in the smallest possible amount of time," irrespective of what is to be seen along the way, like the London lady, who, when crossing the Simplon, was occupied with one of Bulwer's novels.

The number of books, descriptive of places in the North West Provinces, is quite puzzling to a traveller, and almost all are, to a great extent, echoes of *Heber's Journal,* which stands pre-eminently the *Magnum opus* as the guide to the traveller in India. His descriptions are generally accurate and true, and, to a great degee, they are suited for 1853. Some slight mistakes occur here and there, which, it is to be regretted, were not corrected by Murray, when he brought out his cheap edition of *Heber* in the Colonial Library. Among the Foreigners who have visited India, we notice *Monsieur Theroulde,* who travelled in 1838—40, *" dans l' interet des etudes literaires et archeologiques de l' Inde ancienne:"* he proceeded as far as Kashmir, and has given us in a volume, 12mo., pp. 252, a lively sketch of what he saw. *Captain Von Orlich* came to India to learn the art of war, as in former days young gentlemen visited the Low Countries for a similar purpose; but the Seikh war was all over when he arrived; he has given us, however, an interesting series of letters on India, addressed to Ritter and Humboldt. *Signor Manoulie* was forty-eight years Court Physician at Delhi, in Aurungzebe's time, and has handed down to us a very vivid account. *Honigberger's Thirty-five Years in the East* is valuable for medical men—he was physician at the Seikh Court. Foreigners do not give us as many gossiping accounts of dinners and hunting parties as English writers do; but we get a better description of the country. What English writer, excepting Heber, is to be compared to *Dr. Hoffmeister*, who accompanied Prince Waldemar of Prussia to India in 1845, and has given us such a full detail of what he saw? *Schomberg's Travels in India and Kashmir*—a few years since—alluded to in another place in the present No.—are also useful.

Among the works of modern English tourists, are Lieut. Bacon's *First Impressions*, 1831 to 1836, written in a lively style, describing a sporting life in the North West Provinces, giving a good account of Delhi, Agra, &c.; *Parbury's Hand-Book; Major Archer's Tour,* 1828; *Stocqueler's Hand-Book of India,* 1844, is the work of a practical man, who gives a considerable amount of information. *Mundy's Pen and Pencil Sketches,* 1828—*Skinner's Excursions in India, in* 1826—*Sleeman's Rambles and Recollections of an Indian Official,* 1844, abound with lively sketches of the peasantry and their customs.

Nor have ladies' pens been idle; we have a *Narrative of a Three Months' March in India, in* 1833, by the wife of an officer, giving a full detail of the roughing it on a march, breakage, &c. &c.: she went no higher than Cawnpur, the book is meagre. *Mrs. Montanbard's Year and a Day in the East, in* 1844. *Mrs. Parke's Wanderings of a Pilgrim in Search of the Picturesque,*" 2 volumes, 1850, is a mine of information of the most useful kind, abounding in antiquarian descriptions; she is the Lady Wortley Montague of India.

Joseph's Two Maps of the Grand Trunk Road are indispensable—in those are marked the distances, dâk bungalows, chaukies, post offices, &c. *Captain Sherwill's Geological Map* is of the utmost value to every one who takes the slightest interest in the mineral productions of the country. *Daniel's Drawings,* taken in 1788, give a very good idea of some of the magnificent buildings in the Upper Provinces. *Tassin's Map of Bengal and Behar* is good, except that it supplies us plentifully with roads where none such exist—to fill up—just as the Old Dutch filled up the blanks in their maps, by inserting mountain ranges.

There is little instruction or pleasure in visiting places in the North West Provinces, or anywhere else, unless persons are acquainted with the previous history of the localities; without this, the *genius loci* cannot be realized, and the principle of the association of ideas cannot be called into play. The great cities of the North West Provinces are great from their connection with Mogul times; we would therefore recommend to the intending traveller a diligent preparatory study of *Elphinstone's India, Martin's Eastern India, Hamilton's Gazetteer,* and *Macfarlane's Indian Empire.* What interest could Delhi have for a man not acquainted with the history of Timur's successors, the Moguls, who styled themselves " the lights of religion, conquerors of the world"? Just as little as St. Petersburgh could have for one who never heard of Peter the Great, or as the Kremlin at Moscow would have for one unread in the deeds of the old Czars.

Some knowledge of the language is requisite, if the traveller does not wish to be cheated and imposed on. Griffins are considered lawful prey, and interpreters are as bad as the guides on the Continent:—read Baron Von Schomberg's experience on this point. The person who knows Bengali will very soon understand what is said in Hindi, as both are dialects of the Sanskrit.

Though the road between Calcutta and Benares has little historic interest, yet the lover of Natural History, Botany, or Geology, may find many objects to delight him, as the works of Jacquemont and Hooker show—there may be " sermons in stones." Prepared by such studies for the enjoyment of country scenery, the traveller may say, with the author of *Childe Harold :—*

> " There is a pleasure in the pathless woods,
>   There is a rapture on the lonely shore,
> *There is society, where none intrudes,*
>   By the deep sea, and music in its roar,
>   I love not man the less, but nature more.
> From these our interviews, in which I steal
>   From all I may be or have been before,
> To mingle with the Universe, and feel
> What I can ne'er express, yet cannot all conceal."

The French Government have published *Jacquemont's Journals and Scientific Researches,* in 5 volumes, 4to.—Dr. Hooker has also published *Notes of a Tour in India;* he was sent by Government on a botanical mission to India. Sherwill, in his *Statistics of Behar,* gives us a list of ninety different trees and shrubs, which line the forests along the Trunk Road in that Zillah. We hope that the intercourse with the North West

Provinces will lead to a taste being formed for Natural History and botanical subjects, and that the love for country scenery, so natural to Englishmen, will be fostered in India.

Good temper is a great requisite—to allow for contingencies. Our English travellers, who visit Switzerland and the Black Forest, would be often amused at the impatience of your regular Ditcher, when he goes twenty miles from Calcutta: if every thing is not in Chowringhi order, he is highly indignant—Transit and all other Companies have to bear his storm of indignation—he must have his " comforts " everywhere.

The moral and intellectual benefits of travelling is a subject that has been dwelt upon from the days of Cicero to the days of Chesterfield, who enlarges on the benefits of " Le Grand Tour." We cannot make " Le Grand Tour" in India ; but we have the Grand Trunk Road; and we trust that independent of the medical benefits resulting from a change of scene, and relaxation from the ordinary routine of duty—the advantages to be realized from seeing men and manners at large, will serve as a stimulus to our denizens of the Ditch, to enlarge their Indian horizon, and see what India really is—not the Calcutta anglicised type of India " overgrown splendour in squalor," but that presented by the energetic population of the North West, and by the remains of the glories of former days. We write with a most earnest desire to persuade all those who have time and means, to pay a visit to the North West Provinces, and there to gain enlarged views of things, and a nearer acquaintance with the condition of the *people.* The Bengali possesses various good qualities, but if you wish to see a specimen of the real Hindu character, you must visit the North West Provinces—you there see a manly bearing, very different from that of the crouching, sycophant Bengali.

The days when the brandy bottle and the Zenana formed the resource from ennui to the European " exile," are passing away—sights and scenery will give an agreeable relaxation to the Indian resident, whether he be sportsman, sketcher, naturalist, &c.—neither need this relaxation be confined, as heretofore, to a visit " *so far* north as Krishnaghur," or a rustication in Chandernagur.

We hope the Railway will soon carry the traveller quickly over dull parts of the road, that it will be to our Ditchers as the Moscow Railway is to the people of St. Petersburgh ; but our experience from travelling twice through Belgium by Railway is—if you visit a country not as a merchant, but as

THE GRAND TRUNK ROAD—ITS LOCALITIES.

a tourist, the Railways do not enable you to see the land—you are so hurried from place to place, that memory retains very indistinct traces of the peculiar features of the landscape. Our own recollections of Belgian towns are very dim from that circumstance. Besides, subjects of antiquarian or botanical interest can only be examined by slow travelling—one can gain no idea of the contour of a country from a railroad. We passed through some magnificent scenery between Malines and Aix-la-Chapelle, but seen from a rushing rail-carriage, it appeared all tame.

The Grand Trunk Road—the *only* road in the Lower Provinces, after our possession of Bengal for a century—and that not yet completed, eight bridges being wanting between Calcutta and Benares—has cost fifty lakhs. Last century the line of communication with the Upper Provinces lay along the Ganges route, which was adjacent to the old capitals of Bengal, Gaur, and Murshidabad. It was commenced about 1833, and is a noble monument to Lord W. Bentinck. He received the name of William the *Conqueror* from parts of this road being metalled with *kankar !* Its opening has given us a knowledge of the country, like that the Russians have now by the railroad between Petersburgh and Moscow. Previous to his time there was only a road viâ Sulkea, Bankura, Hazaribhag, &c., on which the Government expended several lakhs, now entirely out of repair; it contained no hard material, and was merely a line, marked by two ditches, from which a little earth was occasionally thrown to fill up ruts or hollows made by the rain, while bearers were supplied on requisitions made to zemindars. The present one is thirty feet wide, fourteen of which are metalled, and is forty-four miles shorter between Calcutta and Benares than the old one. Eight rivers, however, still remain unbridged, and we have it on good authority, that three times as much money have been spent on the construction of the road in the Lower Provinces, as ought to have sufficed for completing those bridges and keeping the road in thorough repair. It was under the Military Board.

Not only is the Trunk Road a scene for tourists, but it also presents another subject of interest. We believe, notwithstanding Calcutta prejudices to the contrary, that Bombay is destined to be the great steam-port of India, and that Guzerat will be again what it was in Portuguese and Mogul days, when the little port of Tarda, near Calcutta, was large enough to accommodate the trade with Bengal, while Scinde was the seat of a thriving commerce. The route to Europe, viâ Bombay, will probably lie along part of this line—are we to be always doomed to traverse so many miles to the South, and so many to the North again, rounding Ceylon, &c., in order, after all, to reach the same latitude as that of Bombay? Twenty years hence, we trust it will be done pleasantly, via Mirzapur, Jubbulpur, and Nagpur, or as Mr. Turnbull suggests, by the valley of the Soane, and then along the valley of the Nerbudda or of the Tapti. We are glad to find that the mails between Calcutta and Bombay have, of late, begun to be carried via Mirzapur and Jubbulpur, instead of via Midnapur, the latter route being through a dense jungly country, of no commercial or other importance, and where the coolies are often carried off by tigers, or the letters are reduced to a state of pulp. Even now four days take the traveller to Mirzapur, the Calcutta of the North West Provinces; from thence a pleasant trip along a good road to Jubbulpur, and from that place, on via Nagpur, one can move at his leisure to Bombay.

The Trunk Road to Benares having been commenced only since 1832, and being constructed on the plan of making it as straight as possible, irrespective of towns, there are no cities on the line; you do not meet, as on the old Ganges route, with such places as Murshidabad, Rajmahal, Bhagulpur, Monghyr, Buxar, Ghazipur, yet we trust to show that there are various subjects of interest along this line.

In the North West Provinces police chaukies are located within hail of each other, along every two miles of the road; and in Bengal they have lately adopted this good practice. There is also a *European* overseer of roads stationed at every fifty miles. Medical assistance may be obtained at various places—in fact, a lady may travel along the road as securely as she would along the streets of Calcutta, perhaps even more so.

The *dâk bungalows*, the modern form of the Mogul serais, are very comfortable; they line the road at an average distance of twelve miles; between Calcutta and Benares there are thirty-two. Each is provided with two bath rooms, two dressing rooms, and two bed rooms, with bed-steads, while some have more accommodation: hot water, milk, chapatis, grilled-fowl, curry, eggs, are obtainable at all, and in some you may procure mutton, kid, champaigne, beer, &c., &c. Knives and forks, plates, spoons, tea-pots, salt, are furnished in the dâk bungalows, while a khansama, cook, bhisti, mehter, are also provided by Government. Small libraries of religious books are placed in those bungalows located in the North West Provinces, which are very convenient for travellers stopping in them in hot weather. The increase of travellers is bringing those bungalows more and more into demand; European houses cannot now be turned into " Red Lions."

Notwithstanding the complaints made against the Transit Companies, of their occasional bad horses, yet the improvement in travelling effected by them has been great and wonderful. Instead of husband and wife having to be boxed up for sixteen days, in those portable ovens, or coffins, " the conveyance, horsed by man," " horrible boxes, open at both ends," and most thoroughly unsocial, yclep'd palkis, a costly and fatiguing conveyance, shaking your poor bones *quantum sufficit*, travelling at three miles per hour, and at eight annas a mile, and having sleep at night completely disturbed by the bearers at every stage poking a filthy torch in your face and crying out for bakshish; independent of this, lying in an irksome recumbent position, you cannot enjoy the view of scenery or of buildings, cannot well read or have any social intercourse; but the days of palkis, of *demurrages, and dishonest pitarra-wallahs*, are passed—on the whole route from Calcutta to Delhi, we meet with few travellers by them. Old Terry would now rejoice that " men are not turned into pack-horses, a thing most unworthy of a man." There is another mode of travelling—marching *à la militaire* twelve miles daily, having to take a tent, servant, hackeries, utensils of all sorts, with the chance of waking in the morning and finding all your wearing apparel and money carried off by thieves. We know the case of an officer and his wife some years ago, who were sleeping in their tents near *Maharajganj*, beyond Benares. Awaking in the morning, their clothes and all their valuables were gone; the lady had to borrow clothes, and by means of a Government officer they got their keys back by purchase from the thieves! We know another case, of a Missionary, who went to a *mêla* to preach, and while sleeping in his tent at night, the thieves came, robbed him of all his clothes, and he was obliged to go home wrapped up in a blanket. The skilful achievements of thieves on travellers in tents, in this road, as well as in the fortress of Fort William, Calcutta, if collected, would form as interesting a volume as ever did the " Irish rogues and rapparees," or the adventures of Jack Shepherd or Dick Turpin. We can now roll along, by the aid of those Companies, at an average of six miles per hour, or 100 miles daily, allowing four hours' stoppage, changing the position at pleasure, from a sitting one to a recumbent, by drawing a board across the seat: or mount morning and evening on the box, to view the scenery of the country. These gharris serve as sitting-rooms by day, as bed-rooms by night, as a wardrobe, a library, and a kitchen, rendering the traveller independent of hospitality. If detained on the road, you can easily make your own coffee in your carriage, light your lamp and read yourself to sleep. Horses are changed at about every six miles, and coachmen at sixty; there are 156 stages from Calcutta to Meerut, but our ditch traveller must not expect all the conveniences of Chowringhi, he must be prepared, like *all other* travellers, to rough it a little; he must not imagine, that out of 350 horses, which he will employ between Calcutta and Delhi, and back again, *every one* is to be good. There are ups and downs in horses, as well as in life—he must study the doctrine of chances and also the past—think of the time when Benares was a two and half months' journey from Calcutta, by a budgerow, exposed to all the perils of treacherous sand banks, falling in banks, currents, north westers, roguish mánjis who rove a hole in the boat, mosquitoes, fleas and flies, with an occasional day, perchance, on a sand bank; so that the voyage was attended with more risk and infinitely more trouble than one to London from Calcutta, though sometimes these voyages were very social, when " floating villages" of budgerows, those " inverted cocked hats," sailed in company. Read the Journals of travellers on the Continent, thirty years ago, their descriptions of teazing Custom House officers, roguish inn-keepers, bad carriages, &c. When we consider the difficulties those Transit Companies had to encounter, the mortality of good horses in the hills, the badness of the Bengali attendants on the horses, the state of part of the road sometimes, instead of grumbling, we are surprised that they have succeeded so well. In the course of twelve months they will, very likely, fix their head-quarters at Mangalpur, which will possess the advantage of enabling them to control more effectually the most difficult part of the road, the passage through the hills.

The system of travelling by *horse dâk* originated, as almost all improvements have done, in connection with the Government of the North West Provinces. Ten years ago, Mr. Riddel, the present Post Master General of the North West Provinces, and Dr. Paton, late Post Master of Alighur, commenced the plan. Trucks drawn by one horse, and conveying a palanquin, were first employed; but they soon gave way to the convenient palki-ghari; passengers increased, and this led to the formation of the *Inland Transit Company* in 1849, for running a horse dâk on the road. It was started by a native, Tantimul, the famous contractor of the Allahabad and Cawnpur boat bridges. They ran the mails by contract— the original proprietors were Mr. Gee, a Cawnpur merchant, Mr. McLaughlin, Ex-Post-Master of Cawnpur, now Director of the Himalaya Tea Cultivation Company, and

Lalla Tantimul. From Calcutta to Burhi they have nine horses at every stage, six from that to Benares, and four from Benares to Meerut. From Burdwan to Meerut the Company hire horses from sircars at about fifteen rupees monthly; they have reduced their fares in 1852, above Benares, from four annas to two annas a mile, and below, from five annas to three annas. In 1850 Mr. Atkinson started a rival Company, but he soon failed—after him Mr. Probett, of Cawnpur, started a Company; and then the *North West Dâk* Company, a Calcutta Company, *but* well managed, providing excellent carriages, and good horses. This Company employ 600 syces, 200 suwars, 80 native writers, 60 coachmen, and 20 European overseers. Their monthly outlay is 12,000 rupees, their operations extend over a space of 1,200 miles. Such have been the benefits from this horse dâk, that letters reached Calcutta from Benares, all last hot season, in 52 hours, instead of 120, under the old system.

The traveller need not limit his time for a visit to the North West Provinces to the cold weather, for though some delay may arise here and there, in the rains, from ferries and swollen rivulets, yet there is the advantage of a richer vegetation clothing the ground, relieving that arid appearance the North West Provinces have in the cold weather; besides, the horses are not so over-worked by the constant rush of passengers.

We started after the Christmas of 1852, and returned on the 12th of February—we therefore give things as they were then. Since that time several changes have occurred. We mention the places in the order they present themselves on the Map, but would recommend, that the traveller "long in populous cities pent," should, when starting fresh, and anxious for exercise, make a long push, and proceed on at once to Allahabad. With the aid of the Railway, shortly to open to the Mangalpur coal mines, Allahabad may be reached in four days. Taking the average rate of travelling, 100 miles per day, leaving Calcutta early on Monday morning, he may arrive in *Allahabad* on Friday morning, spend a few hours in visiting the fort, &c. *Futtihpur* may be reached by Saturday morning; after a few hours' stay, *Cawnpur* may be reached on Saturday evening, the sabbath rest can be enjoyed there. The traveller may proceed at 4 on Monday morning for *Agra*, where he can arrive on Wednesday night, remain there till the following Tuesday afternoon in the third week, then start for *Delhi*, which can be reached on Wednesday afternoon; remain there till the following Monday, then start for *Lucknow*, which can be reached by Wednesday afternoon; remain there for two days, return to *Cawnpur* by Saturday morning, and the Sunday may be spent in Allahabad; on Monday evening of the fifth week, Mirzapur is reached, and *Benares* on Wednesday; start the following Monday for *Gaya*, reach that on Wednesday, then to *Parasnath* on Friday, and on Saturday night to *Calcutta*.

Starting from Calcutta, we cross the Barrackpur suspension bridge, over a canal which occupies the site of the famous Mahratta Ditch, near which an engagement took place between Suraj Daula and the English, as celebrated in its day as the battle of Aliwal is now. This canal, excavated in 1822, is the grand medium of communication between the Hugli and Eastern Bengal, and is constantly crowded with boats: between 1843 and 1845, two years, 132,230 boats entered it from the Salt Water Lake, and 31,850 from the Hugli at Chitpur, while 107,390 entered Tolly's Nulla within the same period. This canal yields Government a net revenue of two lakhs, of which very little is expended in preventing its silting up, or in widening it in certain parts.

Passing this canal, the Rubicon of Calcutta, we are clear of Calcutta, with its cliques and fetid odours. We meet on the right hand, half a mile distant, one of those towers, erected for the purposes of the great Trigonometrical Survey. Near it, on the right, are the gardens of Budinath Ray, in which an excellent menagerie was kept. Passing various garden houses of babus, and Chitpur, the Northern *Káli Ghat*, noted, during three centuries, for its human sacrifices, stated by Wilford to have been the metropolis of a district in Bengal, we then leave on the right Cox's Bungalow, and the Governor-General's stables. On the left is the road to the Ayurpara school, and to *Kharda*, the residence of the followers of Chaitanya for three centuries.

The road is lined with fine trees, planted by the Marquis of Wellesley, among which are some noble *Acacia, Odina, Melia, Azadiracta*. The first line of Railway proposed, was to have passed parallel to this road, on to the drifting sands of Bhagwangola, requiring a bridge 1,200 feet long, at Ranaghat, and another at Krishnaghur. It is singular how advantages are shifted in Bengal from one locality to another. The left bank of the river has been the favoured side for a century and a half past, now Haurah is to get the preference by its Railway line, and in a few years, the populous districts between Haurah and Hugli, along the line of the Railway, will present as cheering a sight as the Barrackpur road does now.

We pass near *Titaghur*, famous, forty years ago, for its ship-building; but the river is silting up, and ships could not be built there now. Thus, for instance, in the middle of last century, the Dutch used to bring their large ships up to Chinsurah, but owing to the subsequent shallowness of the river, they were obliged to anchor them at Fulta. Beyond Titaghur, openings in the Park present a beautiful glimpse of Serampur. We come next to the Menagerie and Aviary, which will well repay a visit of an hour—the giraffes, bears, tigers, rhinoceroses, &c., &c. We pass along the parade ground, memorable for the execution of the sipahi regiment, who refused, in 1824, to march to Burmah; they were surrounded here, and a discharge of grape poured into them. We come next to the river; on the left are the powder depôts, and to the right is the site of the old Ostend factory, which was fortified in the middle of last century. Near this, Mr. Simms (*Selections from Records of Bengal Government, No. X.*) proposed placing water-works to convey river water to a reservoir between Belgachi and Calcutta, at an expense of seventy lakhs, with an annual expenditure of five and a half.

We pass over *Pulta Ghat* ferry, reminding us of the days when French, Dutch, and Portuguese proas passed by its shores: now the English flag floats alone here. The grounds of Goretti we pass on the right; they once formed the park of the Governor of Chandernagur, and were the Versailles of former days. A mile further on, we come to the ruins of the house, once the scene of revelry and dance, in front of which, last century, 120 carriages have been seen at night, when magnificent balls were given by the French chief to the English élite. We come next to Chandernagur, noted for its healthy situation, with its street on the river side, called by Jacquemont *une délicieuse promenade*; then to the Church of St. Louis, and the Governor's house; turning to the left, we pass close to the ruins of the old fort, battered by the English fleet in 1757; but a guard of twenty-one sipahis, and a few acres of land, are all that remain of the French power in this part of India. Further on, we enter a gate, the boundary of the French territories. What would Monsieur Dupleix say, were he now alive, on seeing the narrow boundary of *la belle France* in India! Next we come to *Bidarra*, where Dutch and English met in the tug of war, (*See Malcolm's Life of Clive.*) We enter Chinsurah, once Dutch; this place had once a fine Dutch fort and handsome gardens, cultivated by the Hollanders—but all has passed away:—they held Chinsurah for 180 years, when they got Java in exchange for it—gold for brass. Passing near the college, originally the residence of General Perron, of Mahratta celebrity, then through a populous street, we arrive at Hugli Ghât ; near this, on the left, was the old fort of the Portuguese, which stood a siege, in 1632, of three months and a half. Hugli was the first settlement of the English in Bengal, who traded here in 1640 ; Aurungzebe cherished a deep hatred against the Portuguese, on account of their buying up children as slaves, to make converts of them, and sell them into distant settlements. 10,000 Portuguese were killed during this siege. Had their countrymen in other places showed the same valour, they would not have had the epithet applied to them of *Gallinas dell' Mar—hens of the sea*. We then pass *Bandel Church*, the oldest Christian Church in Bengal, built in 1599. The monks here saw the capture of the fort, in 1633, which resulted from the explosion of a mine opposite to them. (See *Calcutta Review, No. X.*, pp. 256—259, for a notice of the Portuguese in Hugli.) The English had a factory at Hugli, in 1640.

We pass through the *village of Satgan*, once a royal city, and emporium of trade, and last century adorned with the country seats of the Dutch of Chinsurah. We cross a bridge, over a stream which once held the Ganges waves, when the river flowed down in this channel via Satgan, and came out near Andul, the Nuddea of the South. (See *Calcutta Review, No. XII.*, p. 403.) The first Europeans who came to this country describe two ports, one *Chittagan*, the other *Satgan*. We need not be surprised at few remains of Satgan existing now ; the fate of Gaur, a beautiful city, as late as Akbar's time, larger then than Calcutta is now, but destitute at this time of any inhabitants, shows us the destructive influence of time, and of the climate of Bengal, as well as the effect of river changes.

Leaving Satgan, we enter fairly on the Trunk Road.

The traffic along this road strikes the traveller ; by a calculation made a few years ago, 73,000 foot passengers, 49,000 loaded hackeries, 17,155 empty returning hackeries, 64,415 loaded bullocks, and 339 Government dâks, passed annually between Hugli and Burdwan ; in salt alone, between Calcutta and Burdwan, the trade amounted, in one year, to 12,962 tons. The lake Sambhir, in Rajputana, used formerly to supply salt ; now the Sunderbunds furnish it : the sugar and gur amounted to 18,518 tons. We are glad to find that Government has established, last March, a Bullock Train between Calcutta and Benares.

At *Muggra* we cross over a river in which the waters of the Damuda once flowed—now they join the Hugli thirty miles below Calcutta. The old bed of the Damuda here supplies the Calcutta builders with sand. There is no bridge, and yet there is a surplus of Ferry Funds for the district of Hugli, of Rs. 117,578 ! and from the thirty-one districts of Bengal and Behar, of eleven lakhs !

Mile-stones on the right hand going up, point out to the traveller the distances. We caution him against trusting to natives' estimate of distances, which will be not according to fact; but according to what they think you *wish*. Monsieur Theboulde gives an illustration of this,—walking, near the Ganges, at Allahabad, he asked a native what the name of the river was; he replied, " the Ganges, saheb ;" to be more sure, he asked him if it was not the Jumna, the reply then was, " it will be the Jumna, if the saheb wishes it."

Perua or *Pandua*, forty-two miles from Calcutta, a Musalman village, of 2,000 families, noted for dakaiti, marks the Northern limit of the growth of the cocoanut-tree, which does not flourish beyond this : it requires the influence of the sea air. A tower on the right hand, 120 feet high, is well worth a visit, for the view to be obtained from its summit, commanding a wide extent of country, as far as Hugli. An iron rod runs up to the top, which the pilgrims, who come here in January, say, was Shah Sufi's walking stick. Nearly opposite it is the tomb of Shah Sufi—the leader of the Musalman troops against the Hindus, who on this spot received a defeat as destructive of their sovereignty in Bengal, as Waterloo was of Napoleon's régime. See *Calcutta Review No.* XX., p. 128 : where an account is given of the Mogul translator of Persian documents, at the Court of the Hindu Raja of Perua, having, at a feast given on the birth of his child, killed a cow, and buried the bones, in order not to give offence. But the bones were dug up by jackals, the Hindus rose *en masse*, and demanded punishment on the murderer of a cow—the people seized the child as the cause, and killed it. The Mogul appealed to the Raja—no redress—on this he picked up the bones and went to Delhi; the Emperor sent an army, who defeated the Hindus in a pitched battle. Pandua was at that period a strongly fortified place, the residence of a Hindu Raja. The tradition goes that the place was impregnable against attack, in consequence of a sacred tank, that possessed the property of restoring life to the soldiers that were killed ; but by a stratagem, a piece of cow's flesh was thrown into it, which removed its power. Pandua surrendered, and this tower was erected as a trophy. Shah Sufi was offered the Government of Bengal, by Firoz Taglac, the Emperor of Delhi, his uncle, but he refused, preferring a life of peaceable seclusion in Pandua, devoted to religious contemplation. A fine mosque near it is 200 feet long, with sixty domes, which increase sound like the Whispering Gallery of St. Paul's, London—one part of it is raised, where Shah Sufi used to sit.

On the left hand side, a little West of the village, is a large tank, called *Pir-pukur*, surrounded by *Pir sthans*. There is a fakir here, said to have tame alligators in the tank, that on calling one of them by his name, Fatikhan, the alligator obeys the call, and comes to the surface. We have an account of a similar fact in *Von Orlich's Travels*, where, in a tank near Karachi, he saw thirty alligators, at the call of the fakir, "instantly creep out of the water, and like so many dogs, lie in a semi-circle at the feet of their master." This tank was probably dug 500 years ago; in parts it is forty feet deep: it has a pretty appearance, with the ruined *imambaries* and tombs on its borders, the latter being probably those of Musalmans, who fell in battle at the siege of Pandua: there is abundance of vegetation on its surface.

There is a tank near this called *Shimábasan*, visited by sterile women, who take a *patali* sweetmeat in their hands, dip it in the water, if it floats back to them, they regard it is a sign they will have a son.

Boinchi, a populous village of 15,000 people, is notorious for *dakaiti*—the *patnadar* system, corresponding to the Irish Middle men or Rack Rent system, leads to this. Mr. Dampier, in his last police report, states, that had it not been for the employment given by the Railway embankments, the poverty of the peasantry here would have led to great robberies.

A few miles beyond, we enter the Burdwan zillah, a garden in a wilderness, containing a population of 1,440,000 (see *Asiatic Researches, Vol.* XVI.), one-fifth of whom are Musalmans.

Beyond is *Mimari*, fifty-five miles, likely to be a Railway station. The alluvial soil of Bengal begins to cease, and the land to rise; the streams no longer bear down mud but gravel, the soil becomes sandy, the grass here is a kind of *sachharium*, and forms a beautiful hedge—the *bignonia odoratissima* exhales a delightful perfume, the roads are kept in good order, being metalled with *kankar*, a nodular deposit of limestone, from calcareous springs; it resembles large pebbles, tuberculated on the surface; it binds very well for roads, but forms a disagreeable dust, and after rain, becomes very sticky; it is curious to see in the North West Provinces, gangs of men beating this down, mixed with water, with a wooden mallet, when it speedily forms a surface as smooth as a plastered wall, and as hard as a limestone rock.

At *Dallea Bazar*, the *Damuda* river, a mountain torrent approaches within a few miles of the road, running parallel to it off the left, as far as the Barrakur. It rises in the hills of Ramghur, and drains about 7,200 square miles of country. In the rains as much water falls into it as would fill a channel twenty feet deep and two miles wide. We may judge of the rush of its waters, from the fact, that whereas in the highest spring tides in June, the river at Calcutta rises seventeen feet, the Damuda at Ampta, the same distance from the sea, has only an elevation of ten inches.

Approaching Burdwan by a fine avenue of old trees, we have on the left the Mission Church, erected by the late Rev. J. Weitbrecht, at a cost of Rs. 10,000. The Mission, with its interesting boarding schools, deserves a visit. The tank opposite the church, on the right side of the road, was the receptacle of the bodies of many murdered travellers, in days of *thug* notoriety, when they were strangled on the high road, and their warm corpses were flung into this tank.

The ground beyond was the scene of stirring events. 100 years ago, 120,000 Mahrattas lay encamped here: "those military mushrooms, who spread from the Ganges to the Kavery," rivals first of the Moslems, and who, aided by the French, for forty years contested with England for supremacy in India.

A mile to the left lies the *Damuda*, "une mer de sable blanc," which formerly flowed into the Hugli, by a detour as far South as Bundipur, and then North to Nyaserai; it now disembogues itself near Diamond Harbour, forming, with its barren sands, those shoals, the James and Mary, which threaten, ere long, to block up the Hugli navigation for large ships—the silt held in suspension in the Damuda in the rains is estimated at two cubic inches per cubic foot of water. In the North West Provinces there is a great proportion of sedimentary deposit in rivers—this also comes down here. We need not be surprised, therefore, at the accounts we have of the Ganges in 1794, filling up, with its sediment, the mouth of the Bhagirathi, five miles in length, containing 900 millions solid feet. Respecting these changes, see *Selections of Public Correspondence, No. II, Reports on the Nuddea Rivers.* We have also to calculate on the effects the Gangetic and other canals of irrigation are likely to have on the supply of water which the rivers Jumna and Ganges send to the Lower Provinces. The coal mines give employment to boatmen on this river in carrying 81,000 tons of coal annually to Calcutta, by a detour of 200 miles, at a cost of three annas and a half per maund—its *bunds* have been the great terror of late days, proposed by the Commission of 1836, to be abandoned; but a recent report, *No. XII. of Selections of Public Correspondence,* opposes this view, recommending that the bunds of the right bank be broken down, and that sluices be opened at intervals in the left bank, to drain the water off, and raise the low country by a silting process.

The Raja of Burdwan's palace is well worth a visit of a few hours—he is the richest landed proprietor in Bengal, drawing a revenue of half a million sterling, out of which he pays to Government twenty lakhs. A new palace has been lately erected by him, superbly furnished. He has a fine menagerie, a splendid tank, thirty acres in extent, and spacious gardens. In this place is laid the scene of the popular Bengali poem, the *Vidya Sundara.*

The Raja's family is of Kshetryia origin, but of modern date —the Raja of Vishnupur, in this district, can trace his regal ancestry for 1,000 years. Burdwan has a population of 50,000 : it had the title given to it of *Kusumapur,* or the flowery city.

At *Golgaon,* a few miles beyond the staging bungalow of Sirsole, and twenty-five miles from Burdwan, commences the proposed line of Railway for the " steam port of Calcutta" —Rajmahal, which will then be six hours from Calcutta, by a Railway of 180 miles. The detour of boats in the dry season to Rajmahal viâ the Sunderbunds, is 308 miles. The line crosses the Aji river, a few miles West of Elimbazar, to which large boats can come from the Hugli in the rains. This Railway will enable the traveller to enjoy the views in Birbhum,—the wild and beautiful scenery of the Rajmahal hills,—and to see the remains of Gaur, the Nineveh of Bengal, called by Akbar, the paradise of countries, a city which, three centuries ago, had two millions of inhabitants, and was enclosed by a wall twenty miles in circumference and sixty feet high. The cascade of Mutijirna, and the rocks of Jangira, are also interesting. The whole of a country teeming in the remains of antiquity, so well described by Franklin in his *Jains,* will then be brought to light. Birbhum and Bhagalpur are almost *terræ incognitæ,* while Darjiling, " the natural sanatarium of Bengal," perched 7,218 feet high, will open new views to us regarding Sikhim and Butan :—Sikrigali, Malda, Colgang, Bhagalpur, and its Jain remains, Patarghata, the second Benares, with its sculptures and Buddhist caves—one of which is 136 feet long, and twenty-four broad, without a pillar or beam to support its roof—Monghyr, and Patna, will be accessible. How little do we know of Purnéa, Tirhut, and Rangpur !

Birbhum, the ancient *Mallabhumi,* is quite unexplored : it pays Rs. 750,000 annual revenue to Government, but little is spent on the education of the people, though they amount to 700,000, and yet more than 30,000 bigahs have been given up to *Devatra* purposes. The worship of *Yam*, the judge of death, is extensively prevalent here. The *Santals*, an aboriginal tribe, abound in the zillah. The famous shrine of *Vaidanath* or *Devghur* is in this zillah; its temple, built nearly three centuries since, is a mile in circumference: its mela, in March, is as well attended as any one in India. To the North of it lies the *Jangal tarai*, a wild spot, the lands of which were let out on the plan of Military Colonies, by Warren Hastings, to the veteran sipahis: the aborigines here have thick lips.

A steamer can now go as quickly from New York to Liverpool, as from Calcutta to Rajmahal. The Railway will make great changes in the country. We find that, in three years—from 1842 to 1845—49,209 vessels, paying a toll of Rs. 486,600, passed Jangipur—that in another year, 83,493 tons passed down, 95,373 up the river; and of passengers 31,950 down, and 26,428 up. The majority of these will pour down by the rail, and will render Burdwan and its neighbourhood very different from what they have been. We mention a few statistics to show what changes in the line of traffic are likely soon to occur. The annual commerce of the Ganges from Calcutta to Mirzapur amounts to 1,666,000 tons, and 569,000 passengers; from Delhi to Mirzapur 897,000 tons, and 446,000 passengers. Sugar, 100,000 tons, from the North West Provinces to Calcutta; salt, 125,000 tons, from Calcutta to the North West Provinces. The kankar, limestone, building-stone, and saul timber of the Rajmahal district, will find a good sale in Calcutta; in fact, between the Rajmahal and Currakpur hills, the mineral and other treasures are immense, and only require a means of transit.

Near *Caksa*, at the 102nd mile-stone, the road begins to undulate slightly; at the 110th mile-stone we come to a country yielding a large supply of charcoal; the alluvium is left behind.

At *Kyrasole*, 112 miles, the land is 360 feet higher than the sea level, and the view is picturesque; two spurs are thrown off from those elevations, one in the direction of Berhampur, the other of Nuddea; for a full account of these, see *Williams's Geological Report on the Damuda Valley*. From this place the coal measures of the Damuda valley commence, and extend nearly as far as Bagsama, covered extensively with alluvium, mixed with a nodular argillaceous limestone, called *gootin*, used for building purposes.

Copses, with sandstone peeping out, are to be seen before we come to Mangalpur, reminding one of the Hounslow Heath of former days, though without its highwaymen emerging from the bush. Calcutta Cockneys may talk of the difficulties

C

of our Grand Trunk Road—what would they have said to English roads thirty years ago? Well do we recollect having to travel from London to Bristol, in 1823, on the outside of a mail coach, of a cold November night, right glad to get a seat on any terms, and having the tedium of the way relieved by the guard's anecdotes of highwaymen's adventures on Hounslow Heath, while his full-charged brass blunderbuss showed that the danger had not altogether passed away.

Mangalpur, situated in a vale, memorable for the forays between the different coal proprietors, is the commencement of the coal district. The mines of Raniganj, so called from the Rani of Burdwan having had the proprietary rights vested in her, are between the Damuda and Aji rivers. The history of monopoly in connection with those mines would, if revealed, unfold many a curious scene in connection with the state of law in the Mofussil. They were opened thirty years ago by a Mr. Jones, and deserve a visit of a few hours. Dr. McLelland, in his *Geological Survey*, gives us some beautiful drawings of the fossils of the Burdwan coal. The dâk bungalow here is prettily situated. From the 125th to the 140th mile, the road passes along the Burdwan Coal field: to the left may be seen *Baharinath* hill towering aloft. The Aji river flows to the right at a distance of twelve miles, running parallel to the Damuda; it is navigable, in the rains, ninety miles from its confluence with the Bhagirathi.

By Christmas, 1854, the Railway will be completed. By that time a fine hotel will be established here—which will make the place a kind of Hampton Court for Ditchers on holidays, when, after a pleasant journey of five hours, they will be landed at the foot of the hills, and be able to realize enjoyments to which the denizens of the Mahratta Ditch are now quite strangers.

A little beyond this, the region of the hills begins—the *Switzerland* of Bengal, the future scene of mineral and metallic enterprize for this country. These hills, once the seats of Buddhist shrines and monasteries, with their contemplative residents and chaunting priests, are destined yet to be the abodes of a bustling, noisy, mining population, to be the Cornwall of Bengal, when the name *Kaila Desh*, or coal country, will be much more applicable than its present one, of *Bahar*, the land of Buddhist monks. The Damuda coal field alone embraces an area of seventy square miles, having 300 feet in thickness of coals. Those hills continue for 140 miles, on to the foot of the Dhanwá pass, a land of hill and dale, wood and water, abounding in scenery, interesting to the geologist, and lover of the picturesque; the climate also changes, the nights are cool and clear, the damp and fog of Calcutta are left behind. When the Railway, which, after many blunderings and delays, is hastening to its completion, shall land the inhabitant of Calcutta, who has been for years inhaling the sultry and fetid atmosphere of the Ditch, in five hours, in the land of the mountain and dell—we anticipate a great extension to the pleasures of a residence in India. To the sportsman also it is not devoid of interest, as the district of Pachete, with its trap hills, swarms with tigers and bears, the destruction of which would be a real act of kindness to the defenceless natives. *Palamow, Sirguja, Chota Nagpur,* and *Pachete,* will afford various subjects of interest to the tourist in connection with their aboriginal tribes, primeval forests and rude border chieftains, who, like the lords of the Rhine, or the Rob Roys of Scotland, exercised their predatory habits on all defenceless persons who came within their reach ; and we trust the knowledge of their condition will also call out the sympathies of the Christian philanthropist. There are, in Behar and Bengal, 150,748 villages, two-thirds of which have a system of vernacular education, but based on superstition. Will a Government, which draws a revenue of twenty millions from India, do nothing to give an improved tone to these? The coal mines and Railway, by giving employment, will have a civilizing effect on the people, and will thus give an impulse to education.

We enter now on a new state of things. Instead of the cunning, cheating Bengali, destitute of any real feeling of patriotism, we meet with a nobler and more independent race. The language of Bengal gives way to the Hindi and Urdu, the manners of the people are more manly, frank, and European, the soil alters, the alluvium of Bengal is no more found—eight centuries ago, this country was Buddhist, and Jain monarchs ruled—the language, Magadhi or Pali, a daughter of the Sanskrit, which is now the sacred language of Ceylon and Burmah, was then used here. On this interesting subject much information may be gleaned from *Fa Hian's Travels* in Bengal in the fourth century, published by the Bengal Asiatic Society. (See also the *Calcutta Review, No.* VIII.—*Indian Buddhism.*) The present state of it is as different from the past as is that of Judea now from what it was in the days of Solomon. Bahar is now a place of ruins :—crumbling temples, remains of granite columns, towers, palaces, cities, are found in districts now quite wild and depopulated. Even the site of Palibathra has been assigned to four different localities. Bengal, which in Mogul days was a Botany Bay, is in the ascendant, with its city of palaces *and* hovels, while *Gaya, Rajgriha,* and *Bahar,* are only

names and shadows of the past. Bahar, which once sent
Buddhism from its bosom, supplied Gautama as a law-giver to
Ceylon and Burmah, and became the cradle of Chinese Buddhism, is now " in the sere and yellow leaf,"—but we trust
railroads will open out such a country to the sympathies
of Christian minds—now all is darkness. It sends opium to
poison the Chinese. For an account of the manufacture of
Bahar opium, see *Eatwell's Report, Selections of the Bengal Government, No.* I.

The hills assume a wavy appearance; if one could conceive
one of those immense rollers at the Cape suddenly frozen,
it would give an idea of this swelling of the ground,—the
road reminds one very much of those great military routes
constructed by Napoleon in France. The soil is gravelly,
and only low jungle to be seen, while to the West, conical
isolated hills rise to the height of a thousand feet—a welcome
sight to him who has been " long in populous cities spent."
Along with this the atmosphere becomes more bracing and cool,
and free from the Calcutta damp. Some collieries appear on the
right—symbols of the future changes in this now desolate
district.

The soil is poor, but it contains within its bosom the
germs of great improvement for this neglected country; the
mineral resources will draw European settlers here, increase
trade, schools will rise, and, we trust, the hopes of Christianity
will follow in their train, and that missionaries will take one hint
from the example of the Buddhist propagandists in this country—act more on the agricultural population, and adopt an
extensive course of itinerant preaching. The coal mines will
make the district another Cornwall.

The *Nunia* suspension bridge, a few miles East of Assensole,
is a splendid erection, over a khal which drains 150 square miles
of country.

On approaching the *Barrakur*, the road passes over an iron-
stone district. On the eastern bank, close to the road, are three
remarkable temples.

The *Barrakur* river, a bed of sand in the dry season, but
navigable for boats of 600 maunds in the rains, is crossed at the
146th mile; it divides Pachete from Birbhum. This river rises
in the hills of *Házaribhág*, and crossing the trunk road West
of *Burhi*, runs parallel to it at the distance of fourteen miles
nearly. To the North of it is a fine country, abounding with
rich valleys—a full account of them is given by Dr. McLelland,
in his *Geological Survey of India.* Santals, Lohars, Ghatwals,
and other Hindu tribes, occupy them. Fine timber could be

procured from these districts. Dr. McLelland gives a list of
492 different sorts of plants which he found in this quarter.
The Barrakur joins the Damuda a few miles South of the road.
The Pachete Mountain rises beyond, presenting a noble appearance from the river, towering in its dim outline to the
height of 1,900 feet, compared by the natives to the shape of
an elephant's back.

Taldanga, 148 miles, is near the western limit of the
coal bason of the Damuda valley; to the South of it, a few
miles, are hot springs in a coal district. A short distance beyond
Taldanga, the junction of the sandstone and gneiss rock, forming
the elevated table-land of Upper Bengal, is passed over. The
jungle here is composed chiefly of thorny bushes of *zizyphus*;
the twigs of the *butea frondosa* are covered with " lurid red tears
of lac," which is collected here in abundance, from this plant.
The coal crops out here at the surface, and many fine fossils have
been obtained. According to Everest (*Gleanings of Science*,
1831, p. 133,) these eminences were once, like Europe, islands
of primitive rocks, rising in the middle of a large ocean; the
debris formed beds of humus, out of which vegetables grew and
formed the present soil. As in all coal districts, the soil is
barren.

On a clear day Parasnath can be seen from Taldanga, rising majestically with its conical peak.—The Sinai of the
Jains, being to them what Adam's peak is to the pilgrims of
the Cinnamon Isle.

A few miles beyond Taldanga, we leave the sand-stone, in
which the coal lies, and come to a district of primary rocks—
the roads are mended with quartz. The country still rises,
and hills appear more numerous, until we reach *Bagsama*,
the residence of a Deputy-Magistrate. We catch a glimpse of
Parasnath, towering far above all the minor hills, in the form of
a cone, with a rugged peak. The view is favoured by the clear
dry atmosphere of those regions. Bagsama is right in the
centre of the Tiger district, and is situated in *Pachete,** a *terra
incognita*, having a curious class of aborigines, fond of eating
rats. *Dr. Hooker's Notes* give an interesting view of the
botany and geology of this district.

Fitcori, 170 miles from Calcutta, is 1,050 feet above the sea
level. Five miles from it, at *Rajafuta*, a new road branches
off to *Chota Nagpur*. Another road is being made from *Rajafuta*,
passing *Chakya*, to connect the Chota Nagpur road with
the Ganges at Surajghur. The coal fields at Kahurbali are

* Bagsama is put down in the maps as part of the Birbhum district.

also to be connected with the Ganges by a branch road to Chukra.

A little beyond this we enter the *Ramghur* district, wild and rocky, once noted for the border raids of its chieftains—at the head of whom was the Raja of Chota Nagpur—the road here was dreaded as much by travellers, as Black Heath was in the days of our fore-fathers ; the zemindars levied their black mail, and entrenched in their jungle fastnesses, bade defiance to the British troops. Dr. Buchanan states, that the Cheros, an aboriginal tribe who lived in Ramghur and the Shahabad hills, were " once lords paramount of the Gangetic provinces"—it would be interesting to examine the data for this statement.   This district is rich in iron and coal.

Tope-chanchi bungalow, 188 miles from Calcutta, 1,128 feet above the sea level, lies at the foot of Parasnath.   The scenery around is charming ; in fact, we have seen few places to equal it in this respect ; it is embosomed in an amphitheatre of beautifully wooded mountains.   The traveller should endeavour to leave this place early in the morning, or three hours before sunset, so as to have the pleasure of the views along the road, winding round the base of *Parasnath,* " giant of mountains," which assumes new aspects of beauty and sublimity, according as the curves in the road alter the prospect.   Parasnath will, very probably, some years hence, be a favorite excursion for Calcutta people, when they can steal away for a few days from business, to luxuriate in its quiet and magnificent scenery. Bears abound in the neighbourhood of Tope-chanchi.   Dr. Hooker gives a full account of the botany of the hills near this.

Near the village of *Lal Bag,* beyond Tope-chanchi, ten bearers and a dhuli can be obtained for about five rupees to convey the traveller, through a series of wooded ravines, to the foot of Parasnath, which is very close to the road.   The ascent is very steep and rocky ; and about 800 feet from the top there is on this side a large and handsome temple, with a marble floor and altar, and a hollow dome ; near it is the only spring on the mountain : descending to the North you have a longer distance to go, it is less steep and more undulating ; there are many fine trees, and the views are very grand ; next appears the Jain monastery.   At the foot of the hill, you pass through the rocky beds of dry torrents, amid gloomy glens, over-arched with foliage, with green schist and hornblende shooting up through the ground, while, in the distance, rise the domes of the Jain temples of Muddaband ; near them is a fine banyan, a sacred tree with the Jains. Madavan, a

Jain village, is embosomed in a clearance of the forest, one of those romantic dales, which intersect the ground between the road and the foot of Parasnath, reminding one of a similar romantic seclusion for religieuses at Port Royal, near Paris. The Jain establishment here is much frequented at the season of pilgrimage, in March, when 100,000 people assemble; in the temple is a black image of Parasnath, having seven expanded heads of a cobra as his canopy. Some of the priests have cloths over their mouths, to prevent their swallowing insects, and thus destroying life. This temple was built by Jagat Set, the great Jain merchant of Murshidabad, in the time of Clive, who was worth ten crores of rupees—there is here *Khetraphal,* a deity with a lion's head—we saw the images of Chakreswari and Padmavati also, which are worshipped by the Jains.

Parasnath, a mass of granite, is a spur of the Rajmahal hills, and towers to the height of 4,233 feet. All who have made the ascent unite in enthusiastic admiration of the scenery, in such admirable contrast with the monotonous flat of Bengal. It will be a mighty boon to the people of Calcutta, when they can get to Parasnath in a few hours, at an expense of twenty-five rupees.

Parasnath is the eastern metropolis of Jain worship, as Abu in Rajputana is the western one. Crowds of Jain pilgrims, from all parts of India, resort to this place. They climb to the mountain top, direct from Muddabund, in order to visit the spot where Parasnath, one of their hero gods, obtained *nirvan,* or emancipation from matter. As the Hindus attach great respect to the print of Vishnu's foot, so do the Jains, a sect which arose on the ruins of Buddhism, about the eleventh century, to the foot of Parasnath. For an accurate and compendious account of the Jains, see *Elphinstone's India.* Franklin, in his *Researches on the Jains and Bhuddhists,* gives us an account of Parasnath, with a beautiful drawing of its temple-crowned hills.

The ascent occupied Dr. Hooker five hours and a half, the descent three-quarters of an hour, in a *dhuli,* part of it down stairs of sharp rock.

Parasnath seems likely, ere long, to be famous for the mineral resources in its neighbourhood. To the North of it lies the great coal field of *Kurakdea; Kurhurbali* is to its North-east, having a coal field, four miles from East to West, and two from North to South, 800 feet above the sea level.

On the road to Dumri, may be observed the *cisalpina paniculata* climber " festooning the trees, a magnificent climber, with deep green leaves, and gorgeous racemes of orange blossoms." *Dumri* bungalow, 202 miles,—according to Hooker,

1,429 feet above the sea level, is beautifully situated, surrounded by an amphitheatre of wood-crowned hills of gneiss, horn-blende, schist and quartz; tin ore is found at fourteen miles distant, while at Karrakdya, twenty miles North, immense masses of mica are procurable, which sell for four rupees per maund; three-fourths of the mica used in Bengal is brought from this place. Nilgaus abound in the forests here, the *antelope picta*, about the size of an ox, with sloping back and short horns.

At Bagoda, 214 miles, is the bombax tree with its buttressed trunk; the road winds beautifully along, the hills are clad with *Gemelina, Terminalia, Buchaniana;* " birds abound here, among others, the mohoka *(phœnecopaus tristis,)* a walking cuckoo, with a voice like that of its English name-sake." The views to the East are magnificent.

We come to *Belcuppie*, 226 miles; 300 yards from the road are four hot springs, they rise in little ruined brick tanks, about six feet across. There is a tank here twelve feet in diameter, supplied by a cold spring, which flows between two hot ones; they all meet and flow together into one large tank; one of them is hot enough to boil eggs, and has a horrid nauseous taste, reminding one of the waters of Aix-la-Chapelle—salt is deposited. Dr. Hooker found the temperature of the hot springs to be 169°, 170°, 173° and 190°, while that of the cold spring in their immediate neighbourhood was 75°. Various plants grow in the water. A water-beetle abounded at a temperature of 112°, and frogs were very active at 90°.

The *Burkutta* river is a large stream in the rains, carrying along gneiss and granite boulders.

Barshatti, 240 miles, is noted for its magnificent tope of mango, banyan, and peepul trees: *borassia,* a kind of palm trees, are to be seen here eighty feet high. Their lower part is a short cone, tapering to one-third the height of the stem, the trunk to two-thirds. The Indian *olibanum* tree is here " conspicuous for its pale bark and curving branches, leafy at their apices." A fragrant and transparent gum exudes from its trunk.

Burhi has, three miles to the East, the Barrakur bridge, a noble stone edifice of nine arches, each of fifty feet span. To the North of Burhi are copper, lead, mica, and iron mines. A little beyond Burhi, the road is 1,524 feet above the sea level; we then pass the bed of the Barrakur, a river which is an affluent of the Damuda; after this, excepting the Dhunwa Pass, we have no more of the wooded hills, which continued for 120 miles, indicating thus that the table-land is near its termination.

Near *Champaran*, 257 miles, and 1,526 feet above the sea, is the commencement of the *Dhunwa Pass*. Champaran is 1,311 feet above the sea level: from this the Ramghur table-land, which has had wooded hills for 120 miles, begins to stoop to the Behar plains below, which extend in one uniform level to the foot of the Himalayas. The Dhunwa Pass leads to the valley of the Soane; the road is steep, carried in a zigzag direction down a broken hill of gneiss, six miles, with a descent of nearly 1,000 feet; of this 600 are very rugged and steep, constructed by the sappers and miners in 1836-37. The pass is well wooded, abounds in quartz and felspar; the scenery is picturesque, and quite novel to a Bengali. The following trees are in the passes here:—acacia, butea, cassia, bombax, argemone mexicana, and also the calotropis or purple madar, much used in cases of leprosy. Dhunwa dâk bungalow, 265 miles from Calcutta, at the foot of the mountain, is 1,000 feet below the mountain top, and yet 817 feet above the sea level. The views from it are very beautiful, an amphitheatre of wood-capped hills, the continuation of a chain stretching from Cambay to Rajmahal. The bambu here is green, whereas at a higher level, it is yellow or white— wild peacocks are in the woods—some large and handsome stone bridges are at the foot of the pass, that at Bhawa is a very fine one, and crosses the Mohana torrent with five arches of sixty-five feet span each.

The approach to *Shirgati* is lined with trees of the bombax, acacia, and borassus genera, while here and there the poppy is cultivated: on the tops of some of the hills are to be seen telegraphs erected in the time of the Mahratta war, to communicate between our troops and Calcutta. Shirgati, or the Tiger Pass, is now a poor place, containing 1,090 houses, the largest town on the road next to Burdwan; previous to 1834 it was the civil station—and the old Calcutta road, viâ Vishnupur and the Dhungye Pass, came out here: " tortuous and water worn" the first road was along the Ganges route. It is built on an island of the Fulgo river, which flows from Gaya. The remains of tombs and mosques indicate a period of former greatness, probably in the days of *Shir Shah*, a Bahar man, who became Emperor of Delhi, but did not forget his native country. The town lies to the North of the Trunk Road, near it is an old mud fort, built in 1764. The *Lilajan* bridge, seven miles East of Shirgati, is deserving of notice, built entirely of stone, the largest bridge on the road, having fifteen arches of fifty feet span each.

A road, twenty-two miles long, passable for a carriage, runs from Shirgati to Gaya, the central spot for Hindu and Jain pilgrimage —the paradise of 15,000 priestly impostors, noted for their extortions, tying the thumbs of pilgrims together, who do not yield to their demands. The Government formerly derived half a lakh yearly by the pilgrim tax. It is a singular fact that when Gaya was attacked by the Mahrattas, those priests formed themselves into regiments and repulsed them. Noted of late for its opium cultivation, it is still the Jerusalem of the Jains. *Martin's Eastern India* furnishes a full description of this place, and of the whole district of Shahabad, of the city of Bahar, with its old fort and mosques, and of *Rajgriha*, with its Buddhist caves.

At Shirgati, the old road from Calcutta to Benares, called forty years ago the new road, a curiosity with its bridges, now in the midst of fields, converges, forming from this to Benares one line with the present one ; travellers by dâk, forty years ago, had to hire tom-tom-men to keep off the tigers, while guards were stationed at different places to frighten away the dakoits. When the rail opens out to Patna, the traveller from Calcutta to Delhi coming down might return viâ Patna, Monghyr, and Rajmahal. The population of Patna, in 1837, was 284,132.

Beyond Shirgati, a range of low hills, spurs of the Vindhya, runs parallel on the left; " they are of volcanic rocks, greenstone and syenite, apparently forcing up the beds of quartz and gneiss from below. *Calotropis* and *argemone* are immensely abundant, with a purple *solanum, veronica, anagallis, equisetum, trichodenia indica, boragineæ, labiatæ.*" Gums and medicinal herbs are procured from the woods here, as also the tusser silk from the osan tree ; the shell of the chrysalis of the tusser worm is so strong, as to be used for binding matchlock-barrels to their stocks. Half the area of this zillah is occupied with hills and jungle. In the great famine of 1770, one-third of the population of Bahar died ; men eating men, and mothers their children—hence the jungle encreased from depopulation, as was the case in the Sunderbunds. Round Shirgati, however, 225 villages have been re-peopled.

Madanpur dâk bungalow, 14 miles West of Shirgati, has a picturesque and antique locality ; three miles from it are the temples and ruins of *Umga*, described by Major Kittoe, *(Asiatic Journal,* 1847.) There are fifty-two small temples ; the great temple of Jagannath, 400 years old, is sixty feet high. There are Cufic inscriptions over the gateway—the old ruined palace, tank, and town of Umga—the hills around capped with small temples, are novelties here.

There is a handsome suspension bridge over the Pompon river, four miles East of the Soane ; the village of Seris on the Pompon, about one mile North of the road, is worth a visit, as being most picturesque.

Crossing the Soane, we enter the zillah of *Shahabad*, the ancient

Kikata. A full account of this is given in *Buchanan's Eastern India*, also in *Traver's Statistics of Shahabad*. It contains a population of 1,602,274, yielding a revenue of Rs. 1,394,396 out of 2,425,058 acres, of which one-sixth is uncultivated or unculturable. There are 8,936 villages—no Government schools of any kind.

The *Soane* river, called by Arrian the third in rank of the Indian rivers, is crossed at Barroon, 557 feet above the sea level: we pass it by fording and ferrying ; it takes two and a half hours to go over, being three miles wide ; the ghari being drawn by six oxen through deep beds of sand—a regiment takes twenty-four hours—it reminds one of the sands of the Egyptian desert ; its quicksands are very treacherous: a causeway, 150 feet in length, composed of large slabs of sandstone, is now being constructed, as an experiment, in the middle of the river. The traveller ought to cross either in the morning or evening, so as to have the sublime view of sunrise or sunset behind the Rhotas hills, illuminating at the same time *Rhotas*, once the impregnable fortress of Shir Shah, and *Sasseram* his burial place. The Soane rises in the mountain of Gandwana, from the same fount as the Nerbudda. The Soane, " the only tributary of the Ganges that is not snow-born," has a course of 500 miles ; it was called the *Hiraneyabaha*, by the ancients, who supposed that, like the Tagus, it rolled down sands of gold ; however, pretty pebbles, jasper and agate, are to be found in it, carried down from the Vindyâ hills. (See *Asiatic Researches*, Vol. XIV., p. 399). Though not carrying gold, yet, we trust, the coal mines found out in Palemow, on the *Kayla*, one of its tributaries, will bring in golden treasures. Pliny and Arrian mention this river, and probably, in former days, it may have washed down gold from some California in the hills.

Rhotas, 1,759 feet above the sea, is a spur of the Kymore range, a branch of the Vindya mountains which run from Chunar to Cambay,—the ancient mountain retreats of the Bhils and other aboriginal tribes, their fastnesses against the ruthless arm of Brahminical persecution. Stretching along Orissa, Berar and the Nerbudda, they formed an inaccessible retreat ; the scenery is very fine in the midst of the picturesque valley of the Soane, lined with wooded hills, a favorite excursion for tourists from Mirzapur and Benares. (See *Benares Magazine*, and *Martin's Eastern India*, Vol. I., pp. 432—454, for an account of the Soane valley, and of the ruined palace of Shir Shah, erected 1539, with its high galleries, long cool arcades and terraced walks, embosomed in an amphitheatre of wooded hills.) It has been compared to Rasselas' Happy Valley. Mán Sing, so well known in Bengali history, erected many buildings on it, and it was a place of security for treasure and women: it was a place of refuge for 200 years. Aurungzeb destroyed the idols: see a drawing in *Martin*, Vol. I., p. 439. Shir Shah designed to make his native country the seat of Empire, and Shergar his citadel, but after Humayun's army were obliged to leave Bengal through its unhealthiness, Shir Shah became Emperor of India, in 1540, but Humayun threw all his children from its precipitous heights. Thus ended the Patan rule. Rohitas, who first settled at Rhotas, was an ancestor of the great Rama. Catechu trees abound here, also peacocks.

At the village of *Dhiri*, on the opposite bank, is a lonely grave-yard, which contains the tombs of some Europeans who, probably, met their death in the Soane, which in the rains rolls a torrent three miles wide and ten feet deep. Here horses or vehicles may be procured for a trip to *Rhotas*, through a well-cultivated country. A precipitous cliff, 100 feet high, rises from the plains ; the road in this and various other parts has been raised, in consequence of the fall of water from the hills having been found to have been much greater than was at first thought.

Sasseram, a city of Musulman tombs, has a population of 10,000—Sasseram means a thousand play-things, and is said to have derived this name from a certain Asur who resided there, who had a thousand arms, and on each a different toy. Jungle ceases here, and the scenery is fine, wooded hills and table-land in the distance, but its great object of interest is the tomb öf Shir Shah, the " tiger king." A native of this place, though the son of a Patan zemindar, he rose by his energies to be Emperor of India, in 1540—he lies buried here in the midst of a tank, a mile in circumference, in a tomb composed of a large octagonal hall, covered by a dome, and surrounded by a gallery. His rival, Humayun, Akbar's father, whom he drove from the throne, lies in Delhi. The king is buried in the centre of the great hall, opposite the kibla or prayer niche, having a small column at the head. His favorite officers are buried at their master's feet. A drawing is given of this tomb in *Martin's Eastern India*, Vol. I., p. 425 ; half a mile North-west is the tomb of his son Selim, but the family were killed by the Moguls, and thus the visions of having a second Delhi vanished :—see Elphinstone's Sketch of Shir Shah.

Shir Shah erected a handsome tomb to his father Haseyn ; had he lived, he intended to have made Sasseram another Delhi, and Shahabad the seat of Empire, but Bahar has never risen to note. Shir Shah, however, introduced the rupee coinage, and that still remains. (For a full description of Sasseram and its monuments, see *Martin's Eastern India*, Vol. I., pp. 422—430).

Sasseram has public baths of ancient date.

The Pergannah of Sasseram contains 898 villages, 409,646 acres, of which one-quarter are uncultivated or barren.

From Sasseram to Agra we have the sandstone formation.

Jahanabad, 365 miles, has a serai of brick and stone, built by Shir Shah.

Kharamabad has a mosque, built 250 years ago, by Mir Akbar, collector of revenue in Jehangir's time.

The *Karmanasa* bridge, of free stone, finished in 1831, designed by J. Prinsep, of oriental celebrity, is a noble monument to the memory of the munificent native Raja Putni Mul, of Benares. The same man re-built a temple at Mathura, which cost 70,000 Rs., made a stone tank there at a cost of three lakhs, a well at Jwala-mukhi, which cost 90,000 Rs. : he spent 90,000 Rs. on a Ghât and temple at Hardwar; 60,000 Rs. on a serai at Brindavan : on these and other public works he spent eight lakhs, for which Lord W. Bentinck made him a Raja. He has recorded, in four languages, on this bridge, the fact of his erecting it; the foundation had been previously laid by the prime minister of Puna, who spent three lakhs on it—the sand being twenty feet deep. The Karmanasa flows from the Rhotas Hills, rises thirty feet in the rains, and is 300 feet broad. (See *Benares Magazine,* Vol. II., p. 253, also *Gleanings in Science, October,* 1831.) An account of the Karmanasa bridge is given in the *Calcutta Review,* Vol. V., p. 304.

When we consider the superstitious dread entertained by the natives, of the touch of the *Karmanasa* waters, we can understand what a boon this bridge has been to them. Their *Puranas* state, that when *Ravan* was besieged in Lunka, he was promised deliverance, provided he could bring from Kailas a *linga,* without its touching the ground; he attempted to do so, but Varuna entering his stomach, he felt so unpleasant, that he dropped the linga on the ground, and the impure water which flowed, constituted the *Karmanasa* river, which means merit-destroying, as the *Puranas* state, that though a native, by visiting Benares, is sure of heaven, yet if he touches the water of this river, all the efficacy of the Ganges water is lost. This river rises in the romantic region of the Mirzapur highlands, and has some fine water-falls.

Near the Bungalow are to be seen some mounds in memory of widows burned here.

The *Karmanasa* is the boundary of the Bengal and Bahar Government,—the ancient *Prachii,* whose capital was Pálibathrá (Patna) ten miles, of note even in Greek days, whose dominion extended from Gaur to the Indus. Our recollections of Bahar are painful—the noble country of Bahar, whose energetic population formerly sent Buddhist priests to propagate their faith throughout Burmah, Ceylon, China, Tartary, Nepal and the Eastern Archipelago—is now herself totally neglected by a Christian Government, as far as educational efforts are concerned. *Adam's Reports* on the state of Vernacular education in Bahar, in 1834, present a gloomy picture; since that time no measures have been taken to redress that state of things.

Passing the *Karmanasa* bridge, we enter the jurisdiction of the North West Provinces; it forms the West frontier of Bahar, formerly it was the boundary of the Anglo-Indian dominion. We soon see the vast superiority in point of administration between the North West Provinces and Bengal: everything indicates that the Lieutenant-Governor is acquainted with the condition of the people, whereas in Bengal, Calcutta is taken as the type of the country, and no decided steps have been as yet taken by Government to ameliorate the condition of the peasantry by education.

There are 1,547 policemen stationed on the Trunk Road between the *Karmanasa* and Delhi, not like the old Charleys, to sleep away their time, but located in stations on the road, to patrol all night. (See *Selections, N. W. Provinces*, No. XI., p. 24.)

One signal benefit has been seen from this police regulation of 1848—the land along the Grand Trunk Road has been in the greatest demand, and every sort of produce has risen in value, whereas the localities were formerly shunned by all classes of people.

The difference in elevation of ground between the North West Provinces and "green Bengal" is soon perceptible—in the North West Provinces every thing has a parched-up appearance, the little grass left is dry and withered—water is procured from very deep wells, there are no tanks, and the tall white grass of the North West Provinces shoots out to the height of six feet.

The road approaching to *Benares*, "the classic city of India," a picture in miniature of ancient *Bháratbarsha*, is lined with trees, and soon the river front, forming the outer line of a semicircle capped with temple and tower, bursts on the view— on one side of the river is the old buttressed fortress of Ramnagar, the residence of the Raja of Benares, rising castle-like from the waters; on the other, a crescent of magnificent stone-ghâts, mingled with palace and temple, stretches three miles in extent, and its Tartar edifices, with river banks forty feet high, and Aurungzeb's minarets towering 232 feet, over-looking the trisuls of Siva : reminding one of the descriptions travellers give of the approach to Moscow, and the first view of the Kremlin. At *Raj Ghât* we cross over the ferry; the river here is not one-half the breadth of the Hugli at Calcutta, but is fifty feet deep, rising forty-three feet in the rains, with a current of eight miles an hour; its bed is 300 feet higher than that of the river at Rajmahal, the landing place is steep, and has a melancholy association. In 1850 occurred the catastrophe of the explosion of gunpowder on board of boats anchored close to Raj Ghât, which shattered the Benares hotel to pieces, and blew down various houses which were perched on the bank ridges, fifty feet high. In the hotel two officers were blown out of the window, while the khidmutgar near them, who was drawing a cork, was killed on the spot. On the right is the old Benares fort, which still contains various remains of anti-quity, and probably in former days much of the old city clustered round it. Near it is the Barna, which with the Asi river gave the name Benares; we pass the Benares hotel and the site of the old fort once covered with houses and temples previous to the Moslem invasion. Remains are still found eighteen feet below the surface of the present city. After a country drive of three miles, Benares being on the left, we arrive at *Sekrole*, the Euro-pean station, with its widely scattered European houses. Cac-tuses abound here, being very useful as hedges, as also *parkin-sonia* trees, introduced only thirty years ago from Australia, by Colonel Parkinson, but now extensively grown.

The " Shining city" has been so often described, that we merely refer our readers to *Heber*, or to *Prinsep's Sketches of Be-nares*, 1831; the latter gives us a full detail of the city, with thirty three lithographic drawings and a map. Tavernier describes Benares in 1668, and Heber in 1825, but the city had not greatly changed in the interval. Prinsep gave a census of Benares in the *Asiatic Researches*, Vol. XVII., in 1828, showing a popula-tion of 180,000, of whom one-fifth were Musalmans.

The feeling on entering Benares is very different from that experienced on approaching Calcutta, a half-anglicised city, with its natives on the rage for English imitation in everything. One is here thrown on purely oriental scenes; its 50,000 foreign de-votees give one the different types of the Hindu race. To the reader of the *Kásikhanda*, a mythological history of Benares in Sanskrit and Bengali, Benares calls forth a host of associa-tions.

The city is the paradise of pigeons, and parrots, bulls and beg-gars, devotees and misers; the bulls however are not very annoy-

ing now : its walls, like those of Puna, have " sermons in stones."
The *Chauk* or square is interesting, with its variety of Musalman
slippers, Hindu hukahs, children's toys, Patna wax candles,
Bhagalpur silks, kinkabs, idols, &c.

The *Observatory* rises over the river, and was erected in the
time of Jay Singha, raja of *Jaipur*, in Akbar's days,—no Jaipur
princes, as in Tavernier's days, study astronomy there now ;
the temple of *Visheshwar*, glittering with its gold leaf, rises
near it, a temple which has been enriched in former days by
donations of krores of rupees ; one raja, in 1838, gave half a lakh
of rupees, which he placed on the head of the idol : this temple is
said to occupy the site of the throne filled by Siva 100 million of
years ago. In it are an image of *Surya*, or the sun, with his seven-
headed horses ; there are bells from Nepal ; the holy well into
which Siva is said to have jumped when the Moslems took
Benares; another well, a mineral one, is pointed out, into which
Siva tumbled when he took a glass too much, and tipping his
physician with his drugs over too, he gave the waters ever
since a medicinal taste ; it is called *Gyan Bapi*, being said to
have the power of confering knowledge. *Aurungzeb's* mosque,
built with the ruins of a famous Hindu temple, which he
demolished about 1660, when he displayed his iconoclastic
fury in Benares, and insulted Hindu families, by thus giving an
opportunity of surveying all their terraces. The two *minarets*,
eight feet and a quarter in diameter, are ascended by steep
stairs to the height of 147 feet ; the view from the top is very
commanding, and reminds one of the scene in Le Sage's *Diable
Boiteux*, when the whole city is exposed to view by the demon.

The tanks are interesting from their associations, such as
Manikarna Ghat, adjacent to a tank dug by Vishnu himself, who
obtained, by his austerities here, the privilege of *Mukti* for Benares, the impressions of his foot are still pointed out ;—*Durga-
kund* and its swarms of monkeys ;—the *Mandakini talao*, from
the borders of which a pretty view is obtained—when drained
thirty years ago, 1,500 sacred turtles were found in it, some
weighing 200 lbs. The *Kapildhara talao*, in which the gods
are said formerly to have bathed, the liquid being the milk of
one of the heavenly cows. The *Bukrea khund*, near which the
Hindus probably fought in defence of Benares against the
Moslems, whose tombs are strewed around; the Hindus say
that a girl near this was raised to be a songster in heaven,
for her attachment to a kid given by Siva, while the kid was
born again as daughter to the Raja of Benares.

There are 1,000 temples of Siva, each of which has to be
visited, in order to complete the *Nagar pradakshina*, hence the

proverb to illustrate the prominent features of worship at Benares, Allahabad and Gya, *Kasi hunde, Prayag munde, Gya dunde.* At Kasi, keep moving, at Prayag shave, at Gya pay.

In the *Bengali-tola* there is a Bengali population of about 8,000, they print a Bengali newspaper there, and have two Bengali presses.

But the great modern architectural curiosity of Benares is the Government College, (designed and executed by that zealous Oriental scholar, Major Kittoe, whose recent death has been an irreparable loss)—a gem in building, the finest modern edifice in north India; it cost one lakh and a half, not including convict labor. Its fountains, stained glass, and library rich in oriental lore, will ever render it a subject of interest.

The old Sanskrit college was founded in 1801, January 11. This college was opened by the Lieutenant Governor, Mr. Thomason, a man who has done so much for the people of the North West Provinces, both in education and the improvement of the country. His speech on that occasion was a fine exposition of the sentiments of the enlightened governor.

Benares, the residence of Tulsi Das, the Milton of Hindi, will, we trust, through this college take the lead as the fount for Hindi literature. The pundits here we found to be a superior class of men, they translated for us a portion of *Lewis's History of Philosophy,* into Hindi; and we were quite delighted at the exquisite precision with which they translated the English philosophic terms into Hindi, borrowing from the Sanskrit. The exertions of Dr. Ballantyne, in connection with this Sanskrit College, have been attended with signal success, in proving the use of Sanskrit as an intellectual agent, to bring the science of the Eastern and Western worlds into a closer alliance, and in teaching the pundits to proceed from the known to the unknown. See *Ballantyne's Sketch of the Operations in the Benares College,* 1846-51.

Sekrole is the European station—Buddhist remains have been found here; instead of these we have now there the Church Mission Station of *Sigra,* with its orphan-schools, native Christians, and a Church, the pulpit is finely carved in trellis work. The native Christian women execute neat specimens of worsted work: book binding is also carried on. Part of the compound was once the scene of *thúgi* operations, and in it a deep well is pointed out, into which the bodies of the victims used to be precipitated. See an interesting little work, *Leupoldt's Recollections of an Indian Missionary,* which gives full particulars of this station, and of Benares generally, written in a lively style, full of the details of an experienced man.

Bhelapur was of note in Buddhist times, it was the birth place of the famous Parasnath, who was buried on the mountain which bears his name, and a famous Jain temple is still there; it is now noted for Jay Narayan Ghosal's Free School, founded in 1818, and made over by the babu, a zealous Sivite, to the Church Missionary Society, with an endowment yielding 200 Rs. monthly, the Government giving 250 Rs. more. There are 500 boys in it, and we were glad to see that Oriental studies have their due attention paid them.

Some handsome *Jain* temples are to be seen in Benares, as a number of rich merchants belong to that sect.

Starting for the raja of Benares' country-seat, Ramnagur, four miles from the city, associated with the history of Cheyt Sing and Warren Hastings, we pass by *Durga khand*, noted for its numerous monkeys, which are to be seen in all directions gamboling about. Coming to the ghat opposite Ramnagur, we land close by the buttressed battlements of the raja's castellated palace; the building rises abruptly from the river banks, and has seven courts, corresponding to the seven planets—once designed to have been the nucleus of a city, the rival of Benares, and called Vyás Káshi. Those who die here, are said to be transformed into asses;—hence all the raja's family, when dying, are conveyed to Benares. Two miles distant, in the midst of the raja's gardens, is a Hindu temple, sculptured beautifully in relievo, with images of the Hindu gods and goddesses,—a pantheon in stone, erected by Cheyt Sing;—near it is a magnificent stone tank, made some fifty years ago, by Cheyt Sing, having on one side a beautiful stone pavilion, a favourite spot for picnic parties; persons can sleep here—the river view of Benares is fine from this. This is the most beautiful tank we have seen in North India, its corners are adorned by kiosks, while splendid flights of stone steps on all sides lead down to the water. A Hindu drama, the Ram Lila, is annually performed in these grounds, some of the figures in which are seventy feet high. (See *Calcutta Christian Observer*, 1838, pp. 260 and 261.)

Jaychand, raja of Benares, was killed in battle, by Kutab-ud-deen, the first Moslem invader, who levelled 1,000 Hindu temples to the ground in Benares; this Jaychand was recognised on the field of battle by his artificial teeth, which were fixed with wedges of gold. The present raja's title dates only from 1730, his ancestor being the famous Cheyt Sing of Warren Hastings' days, whose arrest by the latter excited such a sensation, that Hastings had to make his escape out of a window from Benares. Cheyt Sing's father was Bulwat Sing, a fierce ruler, who like an Irish landlord, drove the zemindars away from his estates.

A return from Ramnagur to Raj Ghat will unfold the panorama of the river to great perfection—the *murhis* or cells into which the dying are removed, that their sins to the last moment may be washed away in Ganges water. *Manikarna Ghat,* and the temples built by Alia Baye ;—*Rajrajaswari Ghat,* with its mixture of Moorish and Hindu architecture; the projecting balcony at the *Man Mandal,* the oldest masonry in Benares— the *Dasasvamedh Ghat;*—the gigantic figure of Bhim Sing, who is said to have built Chunar in a day;—conical altars, with the tulsi plant on them;—and the fakirs with their flags supplying Ganges water—all these afford sights of interest. The Ganges has not spared the temples devoted to its worship, the Bazair Bhais Ghat, which cost fifteen lakhs, was swept away by the river sixteen years ago. These ghats and temples may share the fate of Nuddea and Rajmahal, once noble cities, but now entombed in the river.

Crossing over the *Berna,* near which we have a view of the house where Mr. Cherry, in 1799, defended himself single handed for two hours, against a whole host of the Nawab's troops, we pass over the *Pulzaggar* bridge, a fine piece of masonry work and come to the asylum founded by Raja Kali Shankar Ghosal, in 1825 ; he gave 58,000 Rs. to the Calcutta one—the Alms Houses look very pretty. See an account of them in *Selections North West Provinces,* No. XI., p. 59. Passing along the Azimghur road, in a north east direction, we come to the grave yard, which contains some very handsome monuments, erected by Major Kittoe. Here lie the remains of Major Wilford, a man of undying fame as a Sanskrit scholar, who lived at Benares from 1788 to 1822, entirely occupied with antiquarian and geographical investigations in Sanskrit. Beyond is the *Panch kosi,* a road five koss in circumference, surrounding the city, planted with trees and with halting places for pilgrims, who often make its circuit by measuring their own bodies along it. Whoever dies within this boundary is considered sure of heaven, though he be a beef-eater—it is the *via sacra* of the city. We come after four miles to *Sárnáth,* (the Bull Lord), the Old Buddhist Benares ; few remains are now to be found on the spot; it is sharing the fate of Egypt, supplying with its idols the museums of the Benares college, the Asiatic Society of Calcutta, and Major Kittoe's collection. Benares is now the city of 1,000 Sivite temples, the paradise of Brahmans and bulls ; but in the eleventh century its rajas were Buddhists, and Sarnath, with its temples, was one of the head quarters of Buddhism. Even the Hindu *Puranas* admit, that Divodasa, in the days of Náred, introduced Buddhism previous to the war of the Mahabharat, and that subsequently, the Vaishnavas and Shivites carried on a religious war. When Tulsi Das, the famous poet, lived in Benares, A. D. 1574, the site of much of the present Benares was a forest; the decline of Sarnath, and the ascendancy of the Mahrattas, led to the flourishing state of the new city. Excavations are still carried on there by the Government archæologist of the North West Provinces. A brick mound, of conical shape, faced with stones, three feet by two, 9 feet high, is now the chief object of interest, while until lately, numerous statues of men, with flat noses and thick lips, were strewed around. The remains here bear abundant marks of the action of fire, which was very likely applied by the Brahmans, to drive their Buddhist adversaries out; this must have been at a late period, as in 1027 Benares was part of the Gaur kingdom; a Pal prince from Gaur, a Buddhist, ruled and repaired the mound at Sarnath, (see *Asiatic Researches*, Vol. V.) The Musalmans also probably aided in its destruction, as in 1192 Rai Jay, king of Kanauj and Benares, of the Pal family, was defeated by them.[*]

The Trunk Road from Benares to Delhi, a distance of 480 miles, was begun in 1832, under Lord William Bentinck's directions—convict labour being employed; it has few objects of interest; it is as smooth as a bowling green, with a rise of only twenty inches per mile, the want of trees and green verdure to line its sides, forms a marked contrast with the Lower Provinces. You meet with no picturesque plains, no wooded hills, no villages embosomed in palm or cocoanut trees, the greater part is sandy level land, emitting a glare distressing to the eye, though efforts are being made to encourage planting. The young trees are surrounded with mounds of earth, to protect them from the cattle, and in some places a plantain grows close to every tree to cherish it by its moisture. The deep wells indicate the elevation above the sea, the serais in every village note the traffic extensively carried on; crops of cotton, dal, indigo and wheat, are to be seen in their season. The novelties to the resident of Bengal are long lines of camels, led by the nose,—vehicles with wheels made out of one solid mass of wood, like those used in the bog districts of Ireland,—women, like the Egyptian ladies, riding astride on horseback,—cattle drawing

---

[*] The name of Sarnath calls up an association, connected with the name of a man whose death has been an irreparable loss to antiquarian and architectural science,—Major Kittoe, who will be ever recollected in connection with Buddhistical Researches in Behar and Benares. We spent a day with him at Benares, hearing his remarks on Sarnath, and seeing the curiosities he had accumulated from that place and from Bahar: his name will go down to posterity, with that of Prinsep and Wilford.

the water from wells, the water running in channels down an inclined plane, to irrigate the land,—pilgrims to Jagannath,—traders in Ganges water,—cotton clumsily packed in ragged bags, getting dirty and deteriorating every day,—*eckas* or two-wheeled carts,—hackeries drawn by three bullocks, one leading,—the women so much superior to those of Bengal,—the men armed with swords at their side, and a brass-studded round buckler at their back, travellers encamping in the heat of day, by a shaded well,—the bullock waggons of Government, which bring in a considerable profit.

Above Allahabad it is calculated that one million tons of goods, 100,000 passengers by vehicles, and 300,000 on foot, annually pass along the Trunk Road.

Seven miles and a half from Benares, is *Mohun he sarai*, a large serai, presenting of an evening the opportunity of seeing Arab, Cabul and Jain merchants. At *Maharajganj* is a road leading to Mirzapur.

The approach to *Allahabad*, seventy-six miles from Benares, is over a road of boards laid along the sands, and then we enter the *Doab*, the Mesopotamia of the north, across a bridge of thirty-six boats, of 1,000 maunds each, not quite so convenient as that over the Rhine at Cologne. In eleven months in one year, the numbers crossing this bridge, amounted to 435,242 foot passengers, and 33,180 on horses and elephants. The town is straggling, and covers a large space of ground intersected with handsome trees and fine gardens, its main object of interest is the *fort*, built by Akbar in a commanding position at the confluence of the yellow waves of the Ganges with the blue Jumna. Though the *Prayag* of antiquity, there are few ruins to interest the traveller. See *Asiatic Researches*, Vol. XIV., p. 396. The best time to visit Allahabad is in the middle of January, when the pilgrims assemble at the mela held outside the fort, which lasts two months, to bathe in the Triveni and shave themselves—each hair thrown into the water giving them a million years of happiness. Those sands become at this time the paradise of barbers, bringing in a large revenue to them, as no one can bathe until his head and eyebrows are shaved. The pilgrims here are of various castes: *Nagas, Ghosains, Bairágis* and *Sikhs*. Their tents and temporary shops have a picturesque appearance at this time, while across the river, stretch away the shores of Bundelkund,—noted for its diamonds, which are found a few inches below the surface: to the south is the termination of the Doab.

The *fort* taken by us in 1765, now strongly fortified on Vauban's system, was built in 1581 by Akbar. You enter it by a magnificent Grecian gate—the old palace of Akbar remains, and is used as an armory ; the armory room is a magnificent one, 272 feet long, containing 50,000 stand of arms, beautifully arranged in three rows, quite equal in ornamental appearance to the armory of the tower of London.

Adjacent to this, is a place of note among the Hindus, called *Pátálpur*, once perhaps above ground. Guided by a light, you descend into a cave lined with Chunar stone, quite dark, its roof about seven feet high, supported by several hundred pillars, and having in various quarters 1,000 idols—a perfect mythological menagerie and a labyrinth. On the left hand side is the stump of the sacred fig tree named *Akshabat*, which, with its dried up trunk, has stood there several hundred years ; the Hindus say it is a favourite haunt for ghosts, and that the Akshabat tree has been there from the beginning of time, and will remain there for ever. The *Brahma Purana* promises the happiness of heaven to whoever commits suicide, by throwing himself from its branches, and yet Allahabad (Vaisali) 1,700 years ago, sent Buddhist priests to a convocation in Ceylon ; close to it is an aperture in the wall, which, the Hindus say, leads to a subterranean communication between Allahabad and Delhi. There is a large *linga* here. Near this is the famous Allahabad *lath*, or stone pillar, forty-three feet in length, the inscription, inculcating love to animals, and love to another world, on this pillar, was written by Asoka, three centuries B. C.; he was monarch of India, and became a Buddhist. The inscription on it was decyphered by James Prinsep, after it had for ages baffled all native enquiry. It is called by the natives Bhim Singha's walking stick.

The cantonments are four miles from the fort—the garden, spacious serai, and marble mausoleum of Jehangir, son of *Sultan Khasra*, are now in ruins. The temple of Varaha, near the circuit bungalow, deserves a visit.

The Allahabad Mission Press is an interesting object, from the number of vernacular works it has published for the North West Provinces. Notwithstanding its situation, at the confluence of the Ganges and Jumna, Allahabad is quite eclipsed as a commercial depôt by Mirzapur. The population of Allahabad is only 25,000.

The road leading from Allahabad is finely planted, while, perhaps, the finest tamarind trees in India are to be found here —mica is found mixed up with the Doab soil in this district.

Naubaster ke sarai has a large Jain temple.

In *Korah* are a number of tombs, it was once the residence of a Mogul Emperor.

Futehpur, eighty miles from Allahabad, a civil station since 1826, has been noted for its tombs and serais, as also for dealers in horses' skins, who used formerly to poison travellers' horses for the sake of the skins, worth one rupee each, by mixing drugs with the food for horses brought for sale. See *Kinloch's Statistics of Futehpur District*, quarto, a work of 400 pages, giving a mass of most interesting information. We learn from it that Futehpur has grown up during a period of 500 years, that it occupies an area of 160 acres, and has a population of upwards of 15,000 souls ; that it contains 4,181 houses, 306 wells, 7 serais, 46 mosques, and 19 Hindu temples.

Crossing the *Pandua nala,* we enter the *Cawnpur district*, a flourishing one, 10,000 acres of land are under cotton cultivation; it has a population of one million, of which one-twelfth are Musalmans ; there are 16,542 landed proprietors in the district, cultivating 1,495,628 acres, yielding a revenue of 21,47,315 Rs. ; there are 179 Persian, 16 Arabic, 58 Sanskrit, and 280 Hindi schools, conducted by natives. In 1846-7, a calculation was made of the traffic in one year over Pandua bridge, it amounted to 565,347 foot passengers, 40,304 horses, 9,950 loaded bullocks, 62,906 hackeries, and 73,548 camels.

Montgomery's Statistical Report of Cawnpur is an admirable work, a large quarto, containing seventeen maps and ample statistical tables. Cawnpur town, forty-eight miles from Futehpur, stretches the length of six miles, with its immense lines of cantonments, capable of holding 7,000 troops, and garden houses along a sandy plain intersected by ravines ; it was once the principal military station in India, and so was raised from the state of a village in 1778. A population of 58,000. It has many an interesting association for the readers of *Henry Martyn's Life,* or *Mrs. Sherwood's Indian Orphans.* Ice is made here in the winter, in a large field cut into shallow squares, in which broad pans are placed, filled with water, and straw is scattered about. The traveller will meet with dust enough here.

At some leagues distance from Cawnpur, is the place supposed by natives to be the centre of the earth.

The surrounding country produces rich crops of cotton, which now go down the Jumna instead of the Ganges : saddlery and harness are well made here—308 houses are engaged in the trade. Wolves abound.

The Ganges canal debouches at Cawnpur, the road crosses it. A magnificent monument to British enterprise, costing one and a half million sterling, extending 898 miles, and irrigating five and a half millions of acres : it is calculated it will bring in Government a revenue of forty lakhs annually.

A bridge of boats leads to the Oude territory, the ancient Ayudha—Ram's possession. Here the population are armed to the teeth.

Bakauti, a few miles beyond Bilhur, has a curious temple of red sandstone, the exterior ornaments represent crouching tigers.

Six miles east of Kanauj, we enter the *Furrakabad district*, containing a population of 1,003,073, of whom one-eighth are Musalmans.

At *Gursahajganj* dâk bungalow there is a branch road to Fur-rakabad. *Meerun ke sarai*, fifty miles on, is only noted for its once fine serai ; two miles beyond is the Kanauj dâk bungalow ; the route from that to Kanauj, 2 miles, lying across Indigo fields. *Kanauj* is a short distance to the right, the city that pro-vided Bengal with Brahmanical teachers : vast mounds are the only remnants of the glory of a place, the capital of India in Alexander's time, which once contained 30,000 shops selling betelnuts, and was fifty miles in circumference—thieves and sel-lers of fictitious antiques abound there now. Mahmud of Guz-ni laid his desolating hand on it. Many Buddhist coins and relics have been found. In Fa Hian's time one of the towers of Asoka was standing in Kanauj.

At *Bhowgong* the road branches off to Agra. At *Nabigan* we enter the *Mainpuri district*, noted for infanticide. An interesting account is given of the measures of Mr. Raikes, the late magistrate, for suppressing infanticide among the Rajput tribes there. *Selec-tions of the Records of the North West Provinces, No. XI.* We come to the town of *Mainpuri*, the civil station of Etawah, in a sandy plain. An old fortress overlooks the valley of the Esan river, the seat of the raja of Mainpur for centuries, he was a descendant of Prithiraja—" the thunders of artillery an-nounced the birth of a son or nephew of the raja, but the smiles of an infant daughter were never witnessed in his walls"—infanticide was the rule among the Rajput popula-tion. Mainpuri has a Jain temple, and many Játs live near it. A few miles east of *Ferozabad*, we enter the *Agra district*, respecting whose agricultural resources and landed tenures an able report has been given by Mr. Jackson, in his *Statistics of Agra*. *Ferozabad*, forty miles from Mainpuri, abounds in old tombs ; it was formerly walled and an extensive place.

Mahomedabad is ten miles from Ferozabad ; two miles beyond it is a fine temple in a lake, connected with the main land by a bridge of twenty-one arches.

Begum ke serai is within twelve miles of Agra, the Taj becomes visible from this, it reminds one very much of a distant view of the Pantheon in Paris.

The approach to *Agra* or *Akbarabad* is indicated by the hilly nature of the ground, intersected by deep ravines, the abode of wolves; within two miles of the town, on the left hand, the *Taj* lifts its marble columns to view, the link between the past of Akbar's day, and the present of *Kafir* rule. On the right of the road, is the beautiful tomb of Shah Jehan's premier, Etman-ud-Daula, a splendid pile of white marble, delicately carved into fret work, its screens and tessellated enamels were very fine. Near it is the *Ram Bhag*, built by Shah Jehan's empress, on the banks of the river. The Jumna next presents itself, a shallow stream, about ninety yards wide in the cold weather. The traveller crosses by a bridge of boats, 1,256 feet long, and drives on a good road made in the famine year, 1838. Along the left is the quay, with rather handsome ghats; to the right is the commercial part of Agra. Before us lies the fort, built on an eminence eighty feet high, with its red sandstone walls, and Akbar's palace towering over the river, while, between the quay and the fort, is the site of the scene for elephant fights, which were frequently viewed by Akbar and Shah Jehan, from the balcony near the fort walls. The cantonments are two miles from the bridge, and the civil station four miles beyond them. The right banks of the river were formerly the residence of merchants, and contained a large population; they were the Garden Reach of Agra.

Akbar commenced building Agra (previously a village) in 1566, chiefly induced by its central position and navigable river. Some years after that an English factory was established, and we have an account of the famous Tom Corryat studying in it the Persian and Urdu languages, which he spoke like a native, travelling through the country on foot. (*See Calcutta Review*, vol. IX. p. 127 *et seq.*)

Agra is four miles long by three broad, but not one-sixth of its original extent; mounds and old tombs shew what Agra once was, with its 100 mosques, 80 serais, 800 public baths, and 15 bazars. All the existing buildings have been erected from old bricks dug up; it is only of late that bricks have begun to be made—the city is the wreck of the past, with its population reduced from 600,000 to 80,000; the remains of the wall which once environed it, and round which the Jumna's waters flowed, are still to be seen—the modern city has been well named by Jacquemont "une reunion de Faubourgs."

F

The Government college, built in the Gothic style, has a fine quadrangle. The jail contains 3,000 prisoners, among whom are many thugs; the effects of the labors of Dr. Walker, the superintendent of the jail, are most gratifying,—the cheerfulness of the prisoners, though constantly occupied,—the facility with which, under his management, 1,200 prisoners have been taught to read and write Hindi, and thereby have become entitled to certain privileges and indulgences.—The sight of a gang of dakaits marching about, chaunting the multiplication table ;—of felons, after twelve months' study, reading a book in Hindi, and answering simple questions on some of the common objects of nature,—women too answering,—of murderers working at paper-making, weaving, carpet-making, gardening, forging fetters, making military accoutrements,—are not easily forgotten. We see here, and in other parts of the North Western Provinces, an attention paid to the instruction of the lower orders, to which, we are sorry to say, the Government of the Lower Provinces is a total stranger. The school of industry, the convent, and Corrie's college, belonging to the Church Missionary Society, are also objects of interest.

The Vernacular Normal school deserves a visit, a sound education through Hindi is given to the pupils, intelligent young men drafted from the village schools, who here receive a training as Vernacular teachers—they are instructed in Geography, History, Euclid, composition, all through their own language. We may judge of the progress of vernacular education in the North West Provinces, by the *vernacular* course of instruction in Rurki college. Algebra, geometry, mensuration, plane trigonometry, optics, heat, electricity, conic sections, principles of astronomy, are subjects. The Government, as the last vernacular education report shows, are labouring zealously at irrigating the minds of the peasants with the waters of instruction, and by the avidity with which books are bought, we can judge of the results. Ledlie's Agra School Book press shows great activity in the department of vernacular school books, a marked contrast to our Calcutta slow coach, the School Book Society, though having 500 Rs. monthly from Government. Ledlie's press sold, in two years, for the Government vernacular schools established in eight districts, 21,605 volumes; and we may reckon the probable annual sale of vernacular books from it at 30,000. The report on vernacular education, in eight districts of the North West Provinces, embodies most valuable details.

The Roman Catholic burial ground has various curious old tombs, reminding one of Thevenot's days, when in 1666 there were reckoned 25,000 Christian families in Agra;

some of these were Italians, employed as diamond cutters. Among the tombs is one to Colonel Hessing, a Dutchman, built on the model of the Taj, in the Muhammedan style; he was in Scindia's service,—his biography is given in the *Asiatic Register* : he rose from being a common soldier to be Governor of Agra.

The Jesuits here, in Akbar's time, were able men, who could then address the Mogul in his own language. Shah Jehan built a church for them, and two of his brothers were baptized in it.

The *fort* recalls the days of Akbar; it is surrounded by a trench thirty feet wide. We come first to the *Jama musjid*, a large mosque of three domes, with a triple row of eighteen arches, *simplex munditiis* ; then to the hall of audience, 180 feet by 60', now used as an arsenal and armoury, with Chinese and other flags waving in it; the gates of Somnath (!) are at the end of the room, eleven feet high and nine broad, skilfully carved with Arabesques, and bordered with Kufic characters.—They are probably 1,000 years old; for 800 years they formed the entrance to Mahmud of Ghizni's tomb. Here is still to be seen the throne from which Akbar, receiver of a revenue of seventy millions sterling, daily dispensed justice in open court; there is a marble slab also on which the prisoners stood. Terry describes this throne as having a canopy of pure gold, the steps plated with silver, ornamented with five silver lions, spangled with jewels; but the Mahrattas, after the Napoleon fashion, soon reduced things to a simple state.

The *Moti musjid*, or mosque of pearl, along with its surrounding court, and four rows of marble arches, was the private chapel of the ladies of the zenana, formed of exquisitely white marble brought from Jaipur; it was erected by Shah Jehan, in 1656, during the period of his seven years' imprisonment in Agra fort by his rebellious son; each of the slabs on its floor serves as a prayer place. A paper written by a native was here put into our hands, which is as fine a specimen as we have ever seen of oriental exaggeration of description.

Among the objects of interest in the Palace are the *shishah khana*, or bath room, the sides of which were decorated with small looking glasses and niches for lamps, over which water fell in a cascade,—the beautiful verandahs overlooking the river and the Taj, —the small rooms for the zenana ladies playing hide-and-seek —the rooms of retreat in the hot weather—the chamber where ladies were hung, and their bodies dropped into a well underneath (see *Calcutta Review*, Vol. II. p. 411.) The emperor inflicted very summary punishment, almost whipping a man to death, and then making him kiss the rod; sending a man who broke a China cup, to China, to buy another ; burying alive a woman of the harem who kissed a eunuch, &c. &c.

The road from the cantonments to the Taj, was formerly lined with houses of the nobility. This Taj, to the memory of Momtaza Zemami, is the noblest monument ever erected to woman in the world. Momtaza attended to state affairs, while her husband, in company with his French physician, was consuming his hours over the wine bottle; " he raised her out of the dust, from a very mean family." The Taj, one mile from the fort, is not a mere useless monument to the dead; by its exquisite beauty, both of material and structure, it is a school of art, where both the poet and artist can foster a love for the beautiful. Its terraced gardens and orange parterres, kept in good order, are useful for horticultural purposes, while there is accommodation for Europeans and pic-nic parties—but the mullah's cry to prayer no longer resounds—no Mogul musicians are here—no Christian is now debarred from seeing the tomb—no eunuch, with two thousand sipahis, any longer guards the approach to a building which occupied, for twenty years, 22,000 men in its erection,—yet the brick scaffolding is said by Tavernier to have cost as much as the building itself, which he calculated at more than three millions sterling. The dome being oval is in the Musalman style, as it is semi-circular in Hindu architecture, shining " like an enchanted castle of burnished silver." It is 260 feet high, seventy feet in diameter, beneath it lies the tomb of Momtaza Zemami, who died in 1621. She was Shah Jehan's favorite wife, a Khadija in her day, the bitter foe of the Portuguese at Hugli. Her virtuous qualities are recorded in Arabic, on marble bedecked with gems. On her tomb is a flower composed of 300 different stones ; all the tombs are surrounded by an elegant screen of latticed marble. Beside this tomb is that of Shah Jehan himself, a man who secured the throne to his own children, from the other members of Timur's house, by the use of the dagger and bow string, yet he himself died a prisoner in 1666. The stillness and dim religious light of the place, and the solemn echo from the slightest sound, are particularly striking. In 1814 the East India Company spent £10,000 on its repairs. Its fountains, eighty-four in number, occasionally play.

The *Ram bhag*, a public garden, is on the opposite side, a beautiful retreat for Akbar's courtiers, who preferred for a residence the cool and quiet banks of the Jumna, to the noise of the city.

On the road to Sekundra we meet with a few of those *khoshminars*, which were the mile stones erected by Akbar, three centuries ago, along a splendid road between Agra and Delhi,

140 miles; at each of those stones was a chaukidar station, while the road was lined with stone aqueducts for irrigation, and shaded with magnificent evergreen trees, brought in full growth by elephants from the forests. It formed part of the great road to Lahore, called by travellers the long walk.

Sekundra, or the city of Alexander, six miles from Agra fort, contains the tomb of Akbar; his noble dust lies in a vault here, since 1605, when he died, after a happy reign of fifty years. The mausoleum was begun by him and finished by his son. It is four storeys high, each story diminishing in height. From its roof, composed of beautiful white marble, exquisitely carved, you enjoy a fine view of Agra, the city of his creation. Akbar's tombstone is on the lower story, elegantly carved in devices of flower wreaths, with the word Akbar inwrought, while his title is given in the following language, "light of heaven! right hand of the Almighty!" on the top over it, are inscribed the ninety-nine attributes of God from the *Koran*. The verandas of this tomb are so large as to have once served as barracks to a regiment of dragoons.

From Akbar's tomb we come to the Church Mission Station of Sekundra, which provides the comforts of a religion which Akbar highly esteemed. The *Sekundra Press*, the largest in India, was founded by the Church Missionary Society, and located in a tomb erected by Akbar, over the remains of Munni Begum, a Christian, one of his wives,—one out of 5,000. The tomb afforded shelter to 300 orphans in the famine of 1837.

Agra is a Muhammedan city,—the person in search of Hindu antiquities must visit *Muthura and Brindaban,*—to see the ghat in the latter place where Krishna killed the snake, the tree in which he played the flute, from whose withered branches hang ribbons, to represent the milkmaids' dresses which he stole. Brindabun is noted as the paradise of apes, peacocks, and fishes: handsome ghats line the river Jumna. It has two fine temples of red stone, one of them in the form of a Greek cross. *Mathura* had in Tavernier's time an hospital for apes; it still possesses various fine buildings, the remains of what was plundered by Mahmud of Ghizni, who took away 300 camels' loads of silver from it.

It is a singular fact, illustrating the forbearance of the Moguls and the stability of the Hindu village communities, that around Agra, though the seat of Moslem Government, hardly an instance occurs of a Musalman claiming hereditary property in the soil, while many Hindus can show that their ancestors occupied the villages for twenty centuries.

The neighbourhood of Agra abounds in objects of interest.

Dig, with its fine palace ;—*Bhurtpur*, famous for its siege, but more famous now for the beautiful new city planned and finished by the present raja, which bids fair to be the gem of the west.

Futehpur Sikri, twenty-four miles from Agra, was the favourite residence of Akbar, where, amid the delights of his harem, and in the society of philosophers, he laid aside the cares of state ; this Windsor of the Mogul Emperor, erected in 1570, on a crested height, is entered by a gateway 120 feet high, within which is the shrine, made of beautiful marble, of Akbar's father confessor. The *Dewan Am*, or audience hall, where Akbar heard the cry of the poor for justice ; the *Hati durwaza*, a tower said to have been chiefly made of elephant's tusks,—the pulpit, in a mushroom shape, from which Akbar dispensed justice,—the beautiful tomb of Sheikh Selim, who had riches showered upon him, because by his prayers he was said to have procured for Akbar a son.—The marble floor which Akbar used as a Dice Board while women were his counters—(see *Calcutta Review*, vol. II., p. 411)—all remind one how greatness passes away.

On the road from Agra to Delhi, we come to *Hatras*, thirty-two miles from Agra, it had a strong fort, with a ditch 120 feet wide, and eighty-five feet deep ;—bombarded in 1817 by the English, in consequence of its having been the rendezvous of all the thugs and robbers of the district. The native rulers, there, as elsewhere, protected them, in consideration of their sharing the plunder. *Aligurh* is fifty-six miles from Agra : the native name is Coel ; it is noted for its mud fort, which, under General Perron, was a strong fortress : it was taken by Lord Lake in 1803 by stratagem, though it could have held out for a month against a regular attack. Its fosse was deep enough to float a seventy-four, and was in some places 400 feet wide—it was dismantled by Lord W. Bentinck; between the fort and Aligurh, are the ruins of the house which belonged to Monsieur Perron, Scindia's Commander-in-Chief. In Coel, two miles from the fort, is a large mosque. In Abul Fazl's time, 1582, Coel was the capital of a large district. No heads of peasant-robbers, suspended on poles, along the road, now meet the eyes, as in Akbar's days.

Near Delhi we cross a branch of the great Ganges canal, designed to secure 3,320,000 acres from the effects of drought. Delhi is visible twenty miles before reaching it ; the Kutab Minar towers aloft, surrounded by masses of ruins. The city, which once received its crore of rupees in tribute from Bengal, is now bereft of all power,—yet the Emperor styles himself " king of kings."

A fine bridge of boats leads the traveller across to Delhi. A bridge of this kind existed in the Mogul times. Previous to a visit to Delhi, we would recommend the perusal of *Bernier's Travels.* Bernier was a French doctor, and was court physician to Aurungzeb for twelve years, between 1656 and 1668. He lived in familiar intercourse with the Moguls of his day, of whom he has given a faithful portrait. *Sleeman's Recollections* afford valuable sketches of the family of Shah Jehan, as does also *Terry's Voyage to East India.* The author was two years chaplain to Sir T. Roe, Lord Ambassador at the great Mogul's court. Delhi, the ancient Indraprastha, whose origin goes back to twelve centuries B. C. was taken by Kutab-ud-din, a slave, in 1209. Shah Jehan, finding the heat of Agra intense, from the surrounding sands, founded the modern city of Delhi or Jehanabad, about 1628, which soon had a population of one million, now reduced to 138,000. He used the ruins of old Delhi for the new buildings, making it thus the *Dilhi* or heart of his territories. As we approach to the right we have a view of the old walls of Delhi, stretching along the river, in the direction of the English cantonments, two miles distant. They have seven handsome gates; these walls, chiefly of brick, formerly encompassed the city for nine miles, and yet in 1804, they enabled Sir D. Ochterlony to hold out against the whole Mahratta army. To the left we skirt the red sandstone walls of the Delhi fort and palace, and arrive at the dâk bungalow, located " under the shadow of the Great Mogul;" the walls are forty feet high; the fort cost a crore of rupees, inclosing a space of 600,000 yards; adjacent is a ground used in Mogul times for elephant fights and military manœuvres, as also for the arts of astrologers. The ditch was formerly filled with fish, and lined with a flower garden. The old Patan fort of Selimghur, used as a bastille, is joined by a bridge to the new fort erected in 1648, which is surrounded by a wall two miles in circumference, of red sandstone, brought from Bhurtpur. You enter it through a handsome gateway; passing under a fine arcade, you come to what was once the hall of audience, now a lumber room, having still a marble throne, with a pannel ornamented with inlaid work; from hence to the *Dewan khas* or private hall of audience, whose ceiling was once covered with plates of gold, while the peacock throne, valued at seven millions sterling, blazed forth. The throne glistening with the diamond rays, was supported by four massy pillars of gold. Here Nadir Shah drank coffee, while the corpses of 100,000 slaughtered Hindus tainted the air. The *Moti Musjid*, of beautiful marble, was built by Aurungzeb, who has been seen in its fine quadrangle, praying, clad as an old fakir; but the interior now presents only one mass of ruins, weeds, silent fountains, and noisy children.

The *Church*, with its fine dome, was built at an expense of 1,20,000 rupees, by Colonel Skinner, who is interred here, after all his wanderings in the days of border warfare in India (See *Skinner's Life*, in two volumes). This church was erected in consequence of the father having made a vow, that if his son Joseph, who was so dangerously ill, as to be given over by the doctors, should recover, he would found a church as a thank-offering. It is in the Italian style; in it is a monument to W. Fraser, killed by the Nawab Shams-ud-din, in 1835; it cost 10,000 rupees, made of white marble in compartments, inlaid with " green stones, representing the weeping willow."

Close to the church is the *College*, which possesses the best library in the North West Provinces. A portrait of Mohan Lal, once a pupil of this college, is hung up here. The *arsenal* covers several acres of ground.

The *Juma Masjid*, the St. Peter of the Moslems, is built on a rock, the ascent is by three fine flights of forty steps, completed in 1632, by Shah Jehan, after six years' labour, at a cost of £100,000, built of red sandstone. They profess to have in this Masjid a hair of Muhammad's beard, and the Koran of Ali. How different now from the palmy days, when if the Emperor Aurungzeb did not visit it at least once a day, " the shops of the city would have been closed, and the whole kingdom in a state of ferment." A splendid view of the city, as also of the palace, is to be had from the minarets, 130 feet high, enclosing a city in itself ! To the North-west we see the remains of the garden houses of the nobility, while from the garden of Shalimar to the Kutab Minar, a mass of ruins extends for twenty miles; these gardens cost one million sterling, but nothing now remains.

Delhi has not now the fine buildings of Mogul times, —the Omras houses, " erected on a mound overlooking a beautiful parterre, laid out with reservoirs, conservatories and fountains," but neither has it now so many hovels—60,000 thatched houses were burnt down in one hot season in Bernier's time. The Chandni Chauk or place of silver, the chief street, is " the Cheapside," running three-quarters of a mile in extent, fifty yards wide, with an aqueduct in the centre called Ali Mardán Khan's, made in 1626. In the afternoon it is a bustling scene, and gives a good opportunity of seeing native costumes, &c. Midway is the Roshan-ud-Doula mosque, built in 1721, from which, in 1739, Nadir Shah, irritated by a shot fired at him, gave the signal for the massacre of 100,000 people, who were slaughtered in eight hours, in cold blood, by the soldiers,—the plunder he took amounted to forty millions sterling.

Near the college is *Ali Mardan's canal*—Ali Mardan was a noble of Shah Jehan's time—it draws its waters from the Jumna, near Kurnal, 185 miles distant, and was re-opened by Lord Hastings in 1820, at an expense of two and a half lakhs; the inhabitants went out in procession with music, the day it was opened. For an account of this and other canals, see *Asiatic Journal*, 1833, No. 15., *Ditto* No. 171, *for* 1846; *Major Baker's Memoranda of the Western Canals*, which is particularly valuable for the details he gives of the operations for checking the encroachments of the Jumna.

The *College* is on the site of *Dárá's* palace. It has the best library in the North West Provinces, over 9,000 volumes. Dárá, the son of Shah Jehan, had he mounted the throne, might have revolutionized India, as his policy was to confer offices on Christians and Hindus, instead of on mere Persian adventurers; his fate was tragical, his throat was cut by his brother Aurungzeb's order, and his head was presented on a dish to his brother.

The *Museum of the Archæological Society of Delhi* deserves a visit, containing many old coins, curious inscriptions, &c. The Society has published two numbers of transactions, which throw much light on the localities of Delhi.

Passing out of the Delhi gate, you enter on an herculaneum above ground, the ruins of old Delhi, which covered twenty miles of ground—a sea of ruins. The city was destroyed by the Mahrattas, about 1605; in fact, five cities, at different periods, occupied this ground, the old *Indraput.*

Further on, to the right, is the hill on which Timour is said to have stood and witnessed the battle in 1423, when he ordered 100,000 prisoners to be slain in cold blood, the act of one hour:— old Delhi became deserted from that time. The *Observatory* was built in 1730, by the Raja of Jaypur, a famous astronomer, the gnomon is sixty feet high.

The *tomb of Safdar Jang* is four miles from Delhi, a fine building of red sandstone, having a handsome dome, with a beautiful block of white marble in the centre, erected in 1730. Safdar Jang lies in it; he was once a trooper, but rose to be premier of Lukhnow. Rooms large enough to accommodate several parties of travellers, were provided here by a former king of Lukhnow.

G

Half a mile North-west of this, is the mausoleum of Sekander Shah; though he died in 1275, the enamel is still fresh. Passing through masses of ruins, a city of the dead, we come to the *Kutab minar*, the highest pillar in the world, rising with great magnificence to the height of 232 feet. Its section is a polygon of twenty-seven sides, having fifty-four feet in diameter at the base. It took forty-four years in building, and was finished about 1240. It was erected probably as a minar for prayer, by Kutab-ud-din, who rose from being a Turkistan slave, to be the first Patan sovereign of Delhi. Hindu temples supplied the materials. You ascend by 384 steps to the top, from which there is a commanding view—all relics of the past. *See Archer's Tour,* Vol. I., p. 118, and a drawing of it in *Von Orlich's Travels,* also *Sleeman's Rambles,* Vol. II., p. 252, and *Asiatic Researches,* Vol. IV., p. 313. The Government gave very liberally, in 1828, Rs. 22,000, for its repairs. Near it is a magnificent architrave in the Saracenic style, sixty feet high, erected in 1310; ruins are piled all about, probably of Jain origin. Close to it is an iron lath or pillar, thirty feet high, and as many below the ground, believed by the Hindus to rest on the head of their great snake, to have been the palladium of their dominion, and to have stood there 1,500 years.

Toglakabad, a great curiosity, is reached after a drive of five miles from the Kutab, over a hilly road of sandstone; we pass part of the old wall of the city of Jehanpanah. Taglak Shah was assassinated in 1324, but the fort of this city, six miles in circumference, with its enormous blocks of stone and bastions, is a mighty monument of his genius, and of the cyclopean builders; there are many subterranean apartments still remaining. This city, now untenanted, reminds one of those magnificent piles the traveller meets with suddenly in Ceylon or South America. The Moguls, like Nicholas of Russia, were not friendly to the nobles travelling to distant countries, thus spending the money out of it, hence their superfluous wealth was expended on tombs and buildings.

The remains of a covered stone way, of twenty-five arches, leads to the splendid tomb of the founder, with its marble dome: the surrounding plain was once a lake. *Taglak* was killed here by the fall of a wooden house, erected for him by his son; he was a cruel man, and employed much of his time in hunting down the poor peasantry, hanging up their heads as trophies at the city gates. We return from this place to Delhi.

Starting another day from the Delhi gate, we come to *Feroze Shah's lath*, a pillar of Asoka, thirty feet high, twelve feet in circumference, which has stood for 2,100 years, with its inscriptions. (See *Journal Asiatic Bengal*, 1834, p. 105.) The Jats attempted to destroy this by cannon.

Two miles further, the *purana killa* or old fort, a most striking pile, standing out amid the ruins of Delhi, was built by Feroze Shah in 1290, massive, like all Patan architecture, with walls forty feet high, and six feet thick. On the South side are the remains of an amphitheatre, while Shir Shah's splendid mosque, with its horse-shoe-shaped arches, is near the entrance.

One mile further, is the tomb of Humayun, the father of Akbar, 120 feet high. It cost fifteen lakhs, rising from a platform 2,000 feet in circumference. He laid the foundation stone of it himself in 1550; he erected a tomb on a similar plan near it, for his barber, while his family are buried in various crypts in the building, amounting to sixty-eight. The enamel of the mosaic work there is very striking for its freshness after centuries have elapsed. This monument to his glory was his death-scene, he fell from the scaffolding and was killed.

Near this tomb stood *Indraprastha*, or Hindu Delhi, the capital of India twelve centuries B. C.

Nizam-ud-Din's tomb is a quarter of a mile from this. He was an Affghan saint, the disciple of another saint, whose look it was said could turn clods of earth into lumps of sugar. The lattice work is exquisitely fine, and has stood the wear of time uninjured, since 1415. The veranda around it is very handsome, the pillars are finely covered with representations of birds, butterflies, &c.; there are two doors of white marble, also well deserving of notice. Near it is the tomb of his friend Khosru, a great poet. The tombs of the Delhi family are around. There lies, in a marble tomb, *Shah Alum*, whose eyes were bored out by the Mahrattas, when they took Delhi; 300,000 Moslem martyrs are said to be buried in the neighbourhood. Close to it is a *bauli* or sacred tank for pilgrims, into which natives leap from a height of fifty feet for a small douceur.

It would be easy to mention other objects of interest to visit, a short distance from Delhi, such as *Mirath*, which is only 125 miles from the foot of the Himalayas, and thirty-six from Delhi. With the advance of the Railway, Simla can be included in the six weeks' tour. Meerut was a strong place when taken by Timur, in 1399. *Sirdhana*, twelve miles, the residence of the Begum Sumru, noted for the handsome marble altar in its cathedral—*Saharanpur* and its establishment of ghosains and monkeys, and also its excellent botanical garden,—the valley of the Dhun.—*Massuri*, 7,500 feet high, where the ascent into the bracing air causes a proportionate

rise in the barometer of the spirits.—A distant view of Jum-
notri, 26,000 feet high, is to be had here.—*Hardwar*, ninety-
seven miles from Meerut, the place of pilgrimage of 300,000
natives.—*Rurki*, near Saharunpur, noted for its college of engi-
neers.

The limits we have assigned to this article will not allow us
to notice several points of interest for a traveller to the North
West Provinces, such as Missionary and Educational Institu-
tions—the excellent statistical papers published by the Government of Agra—and the Vernacular Press.

But we must return now from the Delhi of the past to Calcutta, and shall notice three places which the traveller can visit
on his return route, Lukhnow, Mirzapur, and Chunar. Passing
through Cawnpur we come to the *Oude territory*, famous for thugi.
Colonel Sleeman has constructed a thugi map of the district,
in which there are 274 stations for thugs. One man confessed
to having been engaged in 931 murders. Lukhnow is fifty miles
from Cawnpur; a mail cart lands the traveller here at the un-
seasonable hour of four in the morning, in the dâk bungalow,
close to the Residency and Post Office; *Lakhnau*, called Lakh-
mavati, from Lakshman, the brother of Ram, dates as a capital only
since 1775, when it was removed from the old capital Fyzabad,
to which a well-planted road leads. The population amounts to
300,000; its buildings are tawdry and showy, not partaking of
the massiveness and magnificence of Mogul times,—plaster and
stucco work; they indicate the waning of the Mussulman power.
The *chauk* is worth visiting as the seat of trade, it is occasionally *decorated* with the heads of refractory zemindars. The
bridge across the beautiful Gumti, the Indian Meander, leads
from the Residency to cantonments; the roof of the Residency
gives the best view of the city, its palaces, gilded cupolas,
and mosques. On the city side is a Hindu temple, elegantly sculptured, the only one which Moslem intolerance will
allow in the city, which gives full license to all dens of in-
famy, but none to any foreign religion. Muhammedanism is ex-
clusively predominant, but its votaries are devoted to sensuality,
not, like the early Kaliphs, to the spread of their faith. The
people met with, show by their appearance the wisdom of the
company in drawing their recruits chiefly from Oude. *Lukhnow*
may be called the paradise of pigeons, who swarm in all
directions.

The *Observatory, Royal printing press, Menagerie, Oriental
library*, are things of the past, the present king being devoted to
licentious pursuits; and in consequence vice displays itself in

the most disgusting forms, while every thing intellectual is neglected.

The *Imámbára* is a handsome building, erected by Asaf Doula, 1784, built after the model of the mosque of Saint Sophia, at Constantinople; it has a splendid hall, 150 feet long, sixty broad, and eighty high; in the centre is the tomb of the founder, with his sword and open koran lying on it; the minarets are beautiful, fluted, and ornamented with wreaths. Near it is the *Rumi durwaza,* or beautiful gate, having over its gate-way the Nawab of Oude's emblem of sovereignty—two large fishes. Adjacent are the royal tombs, enclosed in a handsome court; tigers of green glass, presented by the Emperor of China, and a figure of Muhammad's steed Borak, are to be seen here. An *Oriental bath* is to be had at the Imámbára.

A drive of three miles takes to *Constantia,* the mausoleum of General Martin, who came out to India a common soldier, and died a General; he built this handsome pile intending to sell it to the Nawab, who knowing the General was an old man, did not wish to purchase it, but to take possession of it at his death. The General hearing this, gave orders that he should be interred in a room at the bottom of the house; you are conducted to the tomb by torch-light—where rests an extraordinary man—soldier, gunsmith, watch-maker, and builder at the same time, who often made 500 rupees before breakfast by polishing diamonds.

From Lukhnow we proceed via Gopalganj to *Mirzapur,* noted for its cotton brought from Bundelkund, and carpet manufacture, situated at the termination of the Great Dekkan road, which is splendidly metalled, shooting down like a great artery to Jubbulpur, 239 miles. The approach to it is very beautiful, as it is situated, like Benares, on a fine curve of the river, whose high banks are finely lined with splendid stone ghâts, temples, mahajans' garden houses, having a population of 80,000 residents, likely to increase, and make it, perhaps, the New Orleans of North India. Ten lakhs of maunds of cotton annually pass through Mirzapur, and its magnificent buildings seem to foreshadow its future greatness; among the objects of curiosity are its beautiful *chauk,* lately a noisome tank, its superb *serai* of stone, with towers at the corner, a well and shrubbery in the centre, and accommodation for several hundred travellers, chiefly at the expense of a native lady: —its public *gardens* and swimming baths. New Mirzapur was the ancient *Sagala* mentioned by Ptolemy. (*Asiatic Researches,* Vol. V., p. 2,756.)

The Kymore range of hills and valley of the Soane, thirty-two miles distant, form a favorite excursion for the Mirzapur people; the scenery is very grand, amid Alpine lofty precipices, grottoes, and all the sublime of nature.   See an excellent article on this subject in the *Benares Magazine*, " How we tried to see the Soane."   To the South of the Kymore hills is *Sirguja*, where gold is found in rather large quantities.

A drive out from Mirzapur to a *sanatarium* four miles off, built by a *native*, for the use of *Europeans*, on the brow of a hill, commanding a magnificent prospect, is well worth a visit.   On our way we pass some finely sculptured temples, containing inside a variety of mythological pictures.   On our right lies the temple of Vindya Chal—Kali's Northern residence—the Kali Ghât of the North Western Provinces, frequented by thugs from all parts of India, who make offerings to the shrine here from the proceeds of their robberies and murders.   250 boats of river thugs, in crews of fifteen, used to ply between Benares and Calcutta, five months every year, under the pretence of conveying pilgrims—their victims' back was broken, and the corpse was thrown into the river.   We cross a bridge, which cost 40,000 Rs., built by a Mahant, on the bambu principle, hollow under the roadway, so as to afford accommodation for shops and resting places for travellers, sixty feet over the river, which rises forty-eight feet in the rains, and used to take travellers two hours to cross.

From Mirzapur we proceed to Benares, viâ *Maharajgunj*, and from thence to Chunar.

A drive of two hours, or fourteen miles, along a good road, leads the traveller to the hill fortress of *Chunar* or Chandalgur. A few miles after leaving Benares, we pass over a handsome bridge, which commemorates the name of Prinsep. The Sultanpur cavalry station is within four miles of Chunar, now almost deserted, with its spacious stables and once handsome bungalows; near it is an old mosque, containing the tomb of the Mussulmani wife of an old Colonel, one of the Qui-hies of former days.   From this place a distant sight is had of the Chunar fortress, cresting the Ganges stream, looming in the distance, and gradually enlarging on the view, until after four miles we come to the river, which runs narrow and deep, washing the foot of the rock, which rises 200 feet high. You cross by a ferry, and this Edinburgh Castle of the East unfolds all its massy proportions before you, perched on a limestone spur of the Vindhaya hills, which here descends to the water's edge, while wall above wall rises in tiers before you —there is not another rock between this and the Himalayas. Its military importance has passed away, it is now the Vincennes for the Sikh state prisoners, and the Chelsea of soldiers; it is garrisoned by a few invalids. In former days they excited the spiritual sympathies of Corrie. (*See Bishop Corrie's Life.*)

The fort was built about the eleventh century, by Sultan Mahmud, who, before his descent on Benares, in 1017, fortified it. Since that, its fortune has been various; in 1575, it held out against the Mogul army for six months. In 1764 it was taken by the English. The view from its lofty ramparts is very fine, reminding one of Stirling Castle. By its side is a burial ground, containing some old monuments. Chunar is noted for little now, except its tobacco cultivation, and stone quarries. The *church* is pretty, embosomed in trees. The population amounts to 20,000. Buchanan states that some of the Pal Rajas lived at Chunar or Chandalgur, which would imply that it was a place of some note ten centuries ago.

From Chunar we return to Benares : in a few years we hope the traveller, instead of returning the same way by the Trunk Road, will be able to proceed by rail, viâ Patna and Rajmahal, thus varying the route; and we trust that also the Allahabad and Delhi railway may, ten years hence, be opened. Then the interesting regions of Central India, teeming with recollections of Rajput times and Jain palaces, will form an additional line for tourists, and we shall have the Trunk *Railway* from Benares to Bombay.

SANDERS, CONES AND CO., TYPS., NO. 14, LOLL BAZAAR.